ARCHITECTS WITHOUT FRONTIERS
War, Reconstruction and Design Responsibility

ARCHITECTS WITHOUT FRONTIERS

War, Reconstruction and Design Responsibility

Esther Charlesworth

AMSTERDAM • BOSTON • HEIDELBERG • LONDON • NEW YORK • OXFORD
PARIS • SAN DIEGO • SAN FRANCISCO • SINGAPORE • SYDNEY • TOKYO
Architectural Press is an imprint of Elsevier

ELSEVIER

Architectural
Press

Architectural Press is an imprint of Elsevier
Linacre House, Jordan Hill, Oxford OX2 8DP, UK
30 Corporate Drive, Suite 400, Burlington MA 01803, USA

First published 2006

British Library Cataloguing in Publication Data
Charlesworth, Esther Ruth
Architects without frontiers: war, reconstruction and design responsibility
1. Architecture and society 2. Architecture and society - Case studies 3. Post-war reconstruction
4. Post-war reconstruction - Case studies 5. Architecture - Psychological aspects 6. Architecture - Psychological aspects - Case studies
I. Title
720.1'03

Library of Congress Cataloging-in-Publication Data
A catalog record for this book is available from the Library of Congress

ISBN-13: 978-0-75-066840-8
ISBN-10: 0-75-066840-7

Typeset by Cepha Imaging Pvt. Ltd., Bangalore, India
Printed and bound in the Italy
Index compiled by Indexing Specialists (UK) Ltd

06 07 08 09 10   10 9 8 7 6 5 4 3 2 1

Contents

Contents

List of Figures

(Unless otherwise referenced, the author acknowledges that she has made every effort to obtain permission to publish the following images)

The author acknowledges kind permission of the following to use the images in this book:

Fig. 1.2, Jon Calame; Fig. 1.3, *Journal of Peace Research*, vol. 42, no. 5, 2005, pp. 623–635; Fig. 1.4 from Fred Schwartz Architects; Fig. 2.1 from http://www.english. aljazeera.net; Figs 2.2 and 2.3 from the *Weekly Review* of the construction of Warsaw 22 July 1953; Fig. 2.4 courtesy of Darko Radovic; Fig. 3.3 from www.arch.columbia.edu/ Projects/Courses/Image.schemata/woodsmain.html; Figs 4.1, 4.2 and 8.7 courtesy of Ayssar Arrida; Fig. 4.3 courtesy of Zeina Halabi; Fig. 4.4 Ecochard Archives AKTC; Figs 4.5 and 4.6 courtesy of Solidere; Fig. 5.1 Jon Calame; Fig. 5.2 Cranshaw; Fig. 5.3 UNDP; Fig. 5.4 Yeniduzen 28/1/79; Fig. 5.5 UNDP at http:// www.undp-unops-pff.org/ News.asp?CiD=92; Figs 6.2 and 6.3, Jon Calame; Fig. 6.4. at http:// www.akdn.org/ news/mostar_230704.html; Fig. 8.8, UNDP.

Foreword

After fifteen tumultuous years of war, civil war and ethnic strife since the end of the Cold War, the international community is at last coming to appreciate the absolutely critical importance of effective post-conflict peace-building and national reconstruction. Wounds unhealed and communities unreconciled are the stuff of which renewed conflict is made. We know that the best single indicator we have of the probability of future conflict is the reality of past conflict, with all the unresolved bitterness so often associated with it. Nothing is more important than that ways be found of stepping out of the vicious cycle of recurring violence.

Esther Charlesworth's book is a stimulating and groundbreaking contribution to our understanding of what more can be done to aid this process by a group of professionals whose role until now has been seen in much more limited terms. In the field of post-conflict and post-disaster reconstruction, architects and planning professionals do have an established role: though they are not generally among the 'first responder' teams of medics and relief workers, their task usually has been to reconstruct in the strictest sense, to rebuild the housing and essential service networks that have been destroyed – provided the attention of donors can be sustained, which often, frustratingly, it is not.

Sometimes the architect's role is brought early to centre stage as efforts are made to create strong visual symbols of reconciliation, in ways which may or may not actually aid the peace-building process. The clearest example of such a visible, expensive, understandably ambitious, but in practice rather problematic, international effort – meticulously dissected here – was the reconstruction of Stari Most, the magnificent Ottoman bridge destroyed in the Bosnian civil war. But more often, in the larger and more difficult task of rethinking and re-creating whole complex urban fabrics torn apart by war, architects and planners – internationals and locals alike – have played very much more marginal roles than those of which they are capable.

This book examines how architects and planners can be much more central and genuinely relevant players. One of the most intriguing and exciting conclusions of Esther Charlesworth's research is that post-war urban planning can be a peace-building process in itself. In an increasingly urbanized world, the city often serves as the flashpoint of violent conflict, with rival ethnic and political groups living in close but divided quarters. But just as these close quarters can provide the ignition for conflict, they can also provide an opportunity to prevent its recurrence. By bringing together separated communities to provide a real input into decisions about the most essential reconstruction questions – on everything from sewage systems and road networks to markets and playgrounds and river promenades – the planning process can help build trust and understanding across communities, reshaping not only the physical but the social and political geography of the city.

In our more than ten years of researching and reporting on deadly conflicts and potential conflicts around the world, the International Crisis Group has consistently highlighted the importance of engaging local communities on issues like governance, resource management and the provision of government services. We have recently examined, for example, the case of the divided city of Mitrovica, in Kosovo, where ethnic Serb and ethnic Albanian communities live in bitter hostility on opposite sides of the Ibar river. Promoting the 'softening' of such rigid borders is a slow process but, as we have recommended, maintaining a limited cross-river district as 'a space for unification' housing inter-ethnic institutions and sports grounds, could go a long way to encouraging greater interaction between the two communities and collaboration in city politics. Esther Charlesworth's account here of the Dividing Line Design Studios she orchestrated in Mostar, Beirut and Nicosia, to engage both the public and local architects, planners and students in the creation of these kind of spaces, is a fascinating demonstration of what is possible in very similar situations when professional skills are engaged in this way.

Drawing on the experiences and ideas now captured in this book, Esther Charlesworth founded in 1998 a new Australian-based international organization, Architects Without Frontiers, to mobilize her fellow practitioners to apply their skills on the ground in providing new opportunities and hope for those afflicted by war and natural disaster. Applying the lessons of her research – not least, the critical necessity for projects to be community based so that local participation in physical reconstruction can help build the human capital needed for social reconstruction – the group has already worked on an impressive array of projects, ranging from the post-tsunami reconstruction of schools and mobile libraries in Sri Lanka, to constructing waste management facilities in villages in Nepal, cataloguing the architectural heritage of parts of Afghanistan and rebuilding indigenous housing in Australia.

Esther Charlesworth has shown us, persuasively and impressively, how architects and planners, working with other professionals across multiple disciplines, but above all with local people in their communities, can serve as true architects of peace.

Gareth Evans
President and CEO, International Crisis Group
Foreign Minister of Australia 1988–96
Patron, Architects Without Frontiers (Australia)
Bruxelles, March 2006

Acknowledgements

The real and lasting victories are those of peace, and not of war.

(Ralph Waldo Emerson)

Trying to make sense of cities decimated by war is no easy task. Trying to work out how architects can contribute to rebuilding these cities is even harder. This book is the result of a decade's meanderings across a whole range of urban centres divided and destroyed by ethnic conflict. It seems, in fact, this journey through cities on and past the edge of urban breakdowns has no end.

A whole raft of extremely generous and intelligent individuals have been involved in the book's making. First, I owe sincere thanks to all the residents, politicians, architects and taxi drivers whom I interviewed for this project, many of whose lives were irrevocably destroyed by war. Many of the interviews were undertaken with my colleague Jon Calame as part of another book soon to be released, *Divided Cities*. Ex-Prime Minister of Lebanon Rafiq Hariri (assassinated on 14 February 2005) was one of these many individuals who contributed his precious time to our understanding of Beirut's reconstruction and whose recent death was a huge blow to peace in the wider Middle-East region.

I would also like to thank Miran Rechter, Darko Radovic, Ray Jureidini and Mustafa Madi for their comments on specific case study chapters. All the students involved across the three Dividing Line Design Studios deserve big thanks, especially Beau Beza and Garry Ormston, with whom I set up Architects Without Frontiers (AWF) in 1998. Gareth Evans, who has written the Foreword, encouraged us to set up AWF and somehow we have managed to put a lot of the reconstruction theory, discussed in this book, into actual action!

I am also very grateful to Max Charlesworth and, in particular, John Fien for their continued reading of book drafts and their great support and patience in helping me to get it actually finished.

Finally I owe much gratitude to my editor, Carole Pearce, graphic consultant, Jenine Davidson, and Laura Sacha and Jodie Cusack at Architectural Press.

Esther Charlesworth
Melbourne, March 2006

1

From lines of contention to Zones of connection

Healing wounds and building peace is not the exclusive responsibility of politicians. We, as architects and urban and regional planners, have a major role to play – and a matching responsibility.

(Barakat, 1998: 15)

This book traces my journey as a nomadic architect living and working in cities destroyed by war and ethnic conflict. My specific concern in this investigation is with the role of architects as potential peace-builders in the rebuilding of such cities. The case studies of reconstruction that form the central part of this book chronicle my search for social resonance in the design field, specifically to uncover the roles that architects can play across the broad terrain of post-disaster reconstruction.

Since I began my research on a range of cities destroyed by civil conflict more than a decade ago, the issues of war, terrorism, trauma, amnesia, memory and reconstruction have grown exponentially in the public consciousness. This comes about largely as a result of a tragic global increase in post-Cold War, intra-ethnic and religious warfare and the related catastrophic outbursts of targeted urban conflict and violence. These conflicts include (but are not limited to) the bombing of Belgrade in 1999, the attacks on the World Trade Center and the Pentagon on 11 September 2001, the destruction of the Bamiyan Buddhas in Afghanistan in March 2001, the destruction of Kabul later that year and, in 2005, the demolition of urban and industrial infrastructure in Baghdad.

While some progress is being made in isolated ethnic conflicts, such as the imminent removal of the Green Line barrier across the island of Cyprus and its capital city, Nicosia, newer, larger and even more aggressive barriers are being erected (and in some cases, such as Jerusalem, re-erected) to partition cities in other parts of the world from Lagos to Ahmedabad. The possibility of urban warfare has also become a daily threat through the over-dramatized reporting of 'global terrorism'. Somma comments:

> *War no longer is something abnormal. The subject of war and the city and the various combinations possible between the two terms, war against the city, the city at war with the rest, the city at war with itself, risk becoming mere academic disciplines and fields of speculation.*

(Somma, 2002: 1)

Two related sets of decisions face professionals working in the field of post-war reconstruction. The first rests in the political process of forming new structures of governance in the reconstitution of a 'civil society'; the second decision rests in the type of reconstruction to be followed, that is, will a city be rebuilt along a traditional or a modern style? The first decision relates to whether efforts will be made to integrate the former warring groups under one or several territorial umbrellas, or whether residential segregation will be maintained. This decision is essentially political, but it has critical social implications, and implications for the nature of the planning and design processes to be adopted, the focus of this book.

In the following chapters I examine three case studies: the post-war cities of Beirut, Nicosia and Mostar, and the attempts by urban planners and architects in these cities to reconstruct the urban fabric after the conflicts ended (figure 1.1). My emphasis is upon the socio-spatial effects of war, rather than a detailed analysis of the historical causes of conflict. My aim is not to provide a template for reconstruction: this would be naive and misguided, given the cultural and political peculiarities of each city under examination, and, indeed, of all cities. This investigation is, instead, used to propose a flexible framework to allow architects and other design professionals, such as planners, urban designers and landscape architects (all of whom are referred to here under the collective name of 'architects'), to engage in the processes of social, economic and physical reconstruction. My findings target design professionals wishing to be involved (or who are already involved) in the post-conflict field and/or already engaged in international development projects. They are also of great relevance for design educators, for it is in our universities that the seeds of professional ethics and responsibility need to be sown.

Three case studies

BEIRUT

Capital of Lebanon, where the sectarian bifurcation of the city resulted in its own Green Line or *Ligne de Démarcation* (line of demarcation) into Christian (east) and Muslim (west) enclaves, which only intensified the conflict during the 15 years of civil war (1975–90).
◀ **BEIRUT'S GREEN LINE, 1985**

NICOSIA

Where a Green line or *Attila Line* was drawn across a map of Cyprus in 1963, eventually splitting the island in half between its feuding Greek and Turkish Cypriot population in 1974.
◀ **NICOSIA'S GREEN LINE, 1999**

MOSTAR

Where the Boulevard or the *Bulevar Narodne Revolucije* was erected as a front-line barrier during the war years of 1992 to 1995 and which still largely separates the city along an east-west (Muslim-Croatian) political axis.
◀ **MOSTAR'S BOULEVARD, 2000**

Figure 1.1
THREE POST-WAR RECONSTRUCTION CASE STUDIES

The title of this chapter, 'From lines of contention to zones of connection', provides a context in which architects can assist peace-making efforts in the period immediately after conflict, when partition lines demarcate the boundaries of each warring territory and each party tries to consolidate its shift into its (former) enemy's space. Once an initial political consensus is reached (and there is rarely any point in talking about connection before at least minimal consensus is reached) then the buffer zone along the partition lines becomes the area or zone with most potential for connections. A practical example of such a zone of connection is Rue Monot in East Beirut, which was aligned to the Green Line during the Lebanese civil war, but today is the most popular zone for night entertainment in the country for Muslims and Christians alike.

The main criteria for my selection of the case studies of Beirut, Nicosia and Mostar are, firstly, that all three cities have been divided by a physical partition line; secondly, that all these conflicts have been inter-ethnic in nature; thirdly, that all these conflicts are still unresolved and, finally, that the roles played (or not played) by architects in reconstruction provide a basis from which more general lessons may be derived.

The three case studies (Figure 1.1) also represent different ways that war can divide and destroy a city, historically and physically, as well as a range of design approaches to dealing with the post-war debris. They include:

- *Beirut*, capital of Lebanon, where the sectarian bifurcation of the city resulted in its own Green Line or *Ligne de Démarcation* (line of demarcation) into Christian (east) and Muslim (west) enclaves, which only intensified the conflict during the fifteen years of civil war (1975–90),

- *Nicosia*, where a Green Line or *Attila Line* was drawn across a map of Cyprus in 1963, eventually splitting the island in half between its feuding Greek and Turkish Cypriot population in 1974 and

- *Mostar*, where the Boulevard or the *Bulevar Narodne Revolucije* was erected as a front-line barrier during the war years of 1992 to 1995 and which still largely separates the city along an east–west (Muslim–Croatian) political axis.

While the dividing lines and barriers may have been removed – at least officially – as strategic checkpoints or formal walls in Beirut and Mostar, the book considers why the ethos of partition often remains in the mental maps of residents as psychological fractures and political barriers that loom even greater than they were during the original periods of conflict. For example, a West Beirut (predominantly Muslim area) resident living on the edge of the city's Green Line commented:

> *Do you want me to tell the truth? I don't consider the war over. As long as there are forces outside the Lebanese government, there is going to be a demarcation line. My perception of the situation, being an educated woman, is that the war is not over. The shelling has stopped but the war isn't over. The mentalities are still at war.*[1]

Unfortunately, the reconstruction strategies under investigation in the three case studies include few architectural or urban planning schemes designed to promote the social reconnection of these ethnically partitioned cities. One positive example that will be discussed, however, is the Nicosia master plan project that proposed reconnecting the city by reconstructing the buffer zone and establishing bi-communal communication between the Greek and Turkish Cypriot residents on the island. Ironically, however, the reconstruction plans of Beirut and Mostar have often undermined the goal of long-term peace. For example, the Solidere reconstruction project in Beirut explicitly excluded the Green Line area of the city from its boundaries, even though this former front line of war is right on the edge of the developable land in the reconstruction project.

The patterns of social and economic polarization manifested in physical separation in the politically contested cities of Mostar, Beirut and Nicosia provide a potential future trajectory for many North American and European cities, as will be outlined in subsequent chapters. These post-war environments of sectarian and racial turmoil, pushed right to the fault line of physical partition, can provide profound insights into the fear, separation, violence and alienation that run through most large metropolises. War-damaged cities also force us to explore urban antagonism and tolerance, and to see how designers, planners and policy-makers can contribute practically to the alleviation of racial and social segregation.

Post-war odyssey

My exposure to the infinite dilemmas of post-disaster reconstruction began as a result of a trip I made as one of eighteen postgraduate students at Harvard who took part in a design workshop sponsored by the Aga Khan Trust for Culture in 1994. The workshop, held in Istanbul, focused on the reconstruction of Mostar, a small Ottoman town in Bosnia destroyed by the civil war in the former Yugoslavia. I arrived at the workshop that summer knowing little about Bosnia, the war and how, or even if, architects could be useful in the social reconstruction process after the catastrophe of civil war. Ironically, while we were making seductive drawings of glass and steel structures to replace the fallen Stari Most Bridge, the city was going without water, sanitation and adequate housing for the thousands of refugees then flooding into Mostar. I found one example during my fieldwork in 2000 particularly disconcerting. In Mostar millions of dollars were allocated to the reconstruction of the Stari Most Bridge while the Neretva River flowing beneath contained untreated sewage and hospital waste, making it a public health hazard for the city's residents. In that same year, it was hard to ignore the fact that only 2 kilometres outside the city of Mostar a growing number of war refugees were living in steel container crates.

In time we came to a less naive understanding by listening to personal narratives of war and studying photographs and films of the ruins wrought by conflict in the city. Our growing realization of the stark reality of the violence and destruction of war contrasted sharply with our highly romantic design attempts to reconfigure the city. This experience in Mostar ultimately set me on an investigative path to find more effective models for post-war reconstruction and to understand how architecture can contribute to the social reconstruction of divided societies through the physical reconstruction of urban landscapes and infrastructure.

Subsequent research and project visits to other war-damaged cities suggested to me that many architects working in the field of post-war reconstruction limit their professional roles to reacting to the physical symptoms of destruction without attempting to understand the root causes behind the conflict. 'Symptoms' here are defined as the immediate damage inflicted on cities during periods of sustained conflict, such as damage to the physical infrastructure of their services, utilities and buildings as well as the destruction of iconic or historic structures such as their bridges and religious monuments.

Now, in 2006, more than a decade after my introduction to the destroyed city of Mostar, I continue to reflect on the responsibilities and rights of architects, in both theory and practice, to intervene through design projects within, or on behalf of, communities tragically affected by violence, segregation, urban dysfunction and partition. For example, I have asked myself whether architects should adopt an interventionist stance by taking a professional stand against the violation of human rights and legal injustices caused by civil conflict, and by seeking to use their design expertise to minimize the chances of future conflict? Or is it more ethical to await official commissions for projects to repair the urban fabric destroyed by war? Increasingly, I have come to see the latter as an unprofessional option. However, it is a very common view and was forcefully expressed in a statement from a group of planners and architects I interviewed in Belfast. When I asked about the role of design professionals in the social reconciliation of their still highly fractured city, one senior academic remarked: 'What does planning have to do with alleviating sectarian conflict?'[2]

During my explorations in Beirut, Mostar and Nicosia, I similarly became disillusioned with the activities of many foreign architects invited to work as experts in the postwar field. Generally, they had little experience of working in divided political and physical landscapes and, as a result, tended to produce (and impose) quick-fix design strategies that are attractive to international donors but which invariably denied or, in some cases, accelerated the underlying causes of conflict. It became increasingly disconcerting to observe what might be called the foreign architect's fetish for rebuilding 'cultural heritage icons'. Such an obsession is displayed by local and foreign designers who assume that the immediate reconstruction of the historic core of a war-devastated city (or a historic bridge, such as the Stari Most Bridge in Mostar or Martyrs' Square in Beirut) will restore the city, almost immediately, to its prewar identity and community spirit. Such stances often ignore the fact that the surrounding urban tissue, infrastructure and social fabric are lying in chaos all around them. These architects – and their commercial, political or international patrons – rarely focused on the 'leftover' zones, especially the dividing lines of conflict or the often abandoned and neglected peripheries of the central zones of cities such as Beirut, Mostar and Nicosia.

Related to this deficiency of social and physical analysis in the post-war design field, many design projects in Mostar have concentrated on culturally significant structures, such as the rebuilding of mosques in the old city (Stari-Grad). Similarly, in Beirut, Solidere, the private development company rebuilding the Beirut central district, used 'cultural heritage' arguments to validate its selective reconstruction of Roman archaeological

A   B   C

Figure 1.2
UNDERTAKING INTERVIEWS IN (A) MOSTAR (B) NICOSIA AND (C) BEIRUT

sites in the city's former downtown. This effectively distracted attention from the same company's demolition of much of Beirut's historic centre. The participation of architects in projects such as these raises questions about their professional motivations and led me to wonder whether design professionals may sometimes be even more ethically compromised than politicians and developers since, at least, they ought to know better.

In the early research for this book, my search for effective design processes that could enable architects to contribute positively to the reconstruction of war-decimated cities and the lives of people living in them involved an extensive analyses of secondary data on the history and sociology of the conflicts in each of the three cities and a critical analysis of post-conflict reconstruction processes. It also included interviews with a wide range of actors working and living in the three cities, including taxi drivers and students, politicians and prime ministers (see Figure 1.2).[3] These interviews identified a wide and often contrasting range of views about the impact of dominant and alternative design visions and processes. My analysis of the resulting data provides a rich understanding of the living conditions and reconstruction dilemmas in cities recovering from war and physical and ethnic partition. It is this understanding that underpins and informs the manifesto for an engaged architecture – an 'architecture without frontiers' presented in Chapters 7 and 8.

These data were also used as the basis of a series of academic workshops and 'dividing line' design studios that sought to identify alternative design approaches for the three cities. The design studios involved a high level of collaboration between architectural students, local architects, activists and residents in envisioning design proposals for the buffer zones of the case-study cities. My reflections on the students' engagement with both architectural theory and practice, and the lived experiences of those most affected by the work of design theoreticians and practitioners provide the basis for my recommendations for refocusing architectural education in Chapter 7.

The rise in civil conflict

In terms of the specific rise of civil conflict leading to the reconstruction phenomenon, a few statistics highlight the relevance of this investigation to contemporary geopolitical events.

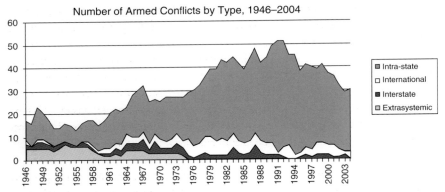

Figure 1.3
THE RISE IN CIVIL CONFLICT (Source: Journal of Peace Research, 2005)

First, the greatest number of civil wars in history has occurred in the past two decades. Since the Second World War there has also been a clear shift in global warfare trends from inter-state to intra-state conflict (Marshall and Gurr, 2003). Fifty-nine of the sixty-four wars occurring between 1945 until 1988 were intra-state or civil wars and during these conflicts about 80 per cent of the war dead were killed by people of their own nationality (Strand et al., 2003). During this same period, 127 new sovereign states have been created and thirty-five new international land boundaries have been drawn since 1980 (Figure 1.3).[4]

Since 2004, there have been thirty active armed conflicts around the globe, many of which are grounded in contested group rights or threatened collective identity. The past five years have in particular witnessed significant inter-cultural hostilities in Sri Lanka and Indonesia (East Timor/Timor Leste and Aceh) as well as Afghanistan, Angola, Chechnya, the Congo, Dagestan, Iraq, Kosovo, Nigeria, the Philippines and Rwanda. While Marshall and Gurr (2003) suggest that the number of such conflicts is beginning to wane, they also suggest that these kinds of inter-cultural hostility are on the increase. Thus, small-scale, non-conventional conflicts – involving groups most easily identified by language, religion or place rather than nationality – have blossomed since the Cold War. These conflicts typically lack uniforms, leaders, rules, treaties, conventions and beginnings or ends. Their seeds are sown in the swampy terrain of cultural identity and its repression and reassertion.

Thirdly, such conflicts now stand as major threats to regional and international security. Marshall and Gurr (2003) has called this trend a third world war, in which insecurity and instability in states leads systematically to violence between rival groups.

While civilian urban populations have been severely affected by this surge of inter-ethnic warfare, they have suffered more recently, in relative terms, than during any other period. In the First World War, for example, about 43 per cent of all battle-related deaths were civilian. That figure rose to around 59 per cent in the course of the Second World War, and since then – during a period when the number of wars within states overtook the number between states – civilian deaths constituted approximately 74 per cent of the wartime totals.[5] The scale and intensity of psychological trauma suffered by non-combatants rises proportionately and post-disaster cities become the arenas of overwhelming loss, dislocation and prolonged anxiety (Calame and Charlesworth, 2006). Vulnerability increases even further for residents of cities that function as an interface for rival ethnic communities in the region.

Finally, these civilian conflicts are being exacerbated by the huge influx of people now arriving in cities, often involuntarily as refugees, especially in poor Southern countries with few economic resources. At the end of 1999, the United Nations High Commissioner for Refugees (UNHCR) reported that there were some 15 million refugees in the world,[6] while other estimates placed the number of displaced persons at between 20 million and 50 million. Thus, nearly three-quarters of the world's refugees have been displaced by ethnic conflicts. The pressure to maintain the physical infrastructure and political administration of a city experiencing such profound urban flux makes cities increasingly vulnerable to internal stress and, inevitably, to civil conflict. These continuing ruptures to the social and fiscal fabric of the world's societies challenge us to rethink not only how cities are to be understood, but also how people are to survive and thrive in large urban centres.

The post-war city as an opportunity

War, disaster gives us the capacity to rethink architecture. Things, buildings will fall apart.

(Woods, 1998: 1)

In Chinese the word 'crisis' contains two interpretative characters. One represents tragedy, the other opportunity. During a period that is technically 'not at war', there may not be the local or international aid funds or incentives to undertake even the most necessary development projects in a city. However, post-conflict, the various forces behind the reconsolidation of a national identity and economic recovery may often turn the rebuilding of a city into an enormous political opportunity. In fact, these forces can drive rapid development, as manifested in the cases of, for example, the phenomenal pace of reconstruction in Berlin between 1991 and 1999 and the speed of Solidere's reconstruction of downtown Beirut between 1995 and 2000. The desire to re-create urban icons with great speed after conflict is also manifested in the more recent events following the destruction of New York's World Trade Center. The ruins of the Center were still smoking with remnant fires when the architects and developers hurried back onto the site clamouring for future commissions and pressuring the city administration to rebuild structures immediately, both bigger and better than the original Twin Towers (see Figure 1.4).

This zeal to rebuild immediately after war occurs because a rapid and radical overhaul of political systems and administrative structures often follows the formal cessation of conflict. New governments and political figures come into power and, faced with economic and physical rubble, governments often seek to present an image of national prosperity, progress and glory by funding large-scale rebuilding programmes. For example, in post-war Lebanon the then newly elected Prime Minister, Rafiq Hariri, used the reconstruction of Beirut as a symbol to re-identify Lebanon as a dominant political force in the Middle East. Hariri had a clear vision that the rebuilding of the Beirut central district would become the future model par excellence, for his united city and country as part of a larger regional plan to place Beirut among other cities on the Mediterranean, at the beginning of the third millennium (Sarkis and Rowe, 1998).

Another driver of reconstruction is the need to re-create and promote new physical symbols and civic icons in a post-war society. Rebuilding the Stari Most Bridge in

Figure 1.4
REBUILDING AFTER SEPTEMBER 11, THE 'THINK' PROPOSAL

Mostar, reopening the Reichstag and repairing the Brandenburg Gate in Berlin during the past decade are prime examples of this. Similarly, as just noted, rebuilding the former central business district of Beirut was intended as an international reconstruction showcase for both the Lebanese public and foreign investors.

Thus, while the aftermath of war is undeniably a time of great physical and psychological trauma, it can also be viewed as a fertile testing ground for political ideologies about the city and a site for radical architectural speculations. While it is logistically difficult to link together urban areas that have been severed after a war, such reconstruction offers a laboratory for thinking about the future form of hitherto polarized urban environments. For example, in Berlin and Beirut at the start of the 1990s, the removal of the physical manifestations of division (the Berlin Wall and Beirut's Green Line) provided the prospect of dealing with physical division and demarcation. As Joe Nasr comments: 'Rather than allow this vital cut to heal by developing a scar on its own, decisions were made in both cases to suture it, that is to surgically, in a planned way, sew torn urban fabric' (Nasr, 1996: 27–40).

However, these decisions about *sewing* the torn urban fabric back together reflect the distribution and configurations of political and economic power. Thus, the models upon which reconstruction in Beirut, Mostar and Nicosia was based reflect the forces dominant in most capitalist cities today. This fact alone may explain the failure of urban and state authorities in these cities to explore alternative approaches to any great extent. Understanding the approaches chosen – and neglected – requires an appreciation of the choices available for reconstruction.

Disintegrating cities

> There is no moral to the story, except a warning to other societies to do their utmost not to reach that state; there are no practical lessons to be learned nor a guidebook for the bewildered to be composed.

> (Benvenisti, 1982: 13)

In a general sense, it could be argued that most architecture is the result of conflict, whether that conflict is in terms of scale, site, budget or programme. Likewise the history of urbanism has been a trajectory of cities 'sacked, shaken, burned, bombed, flooded, starved, irradiated and poisoned' (Vale and Campanella, 2005: 3). However, the traditional planning methods of, for example, imposing fixed master plans in post-conflict situations need to be re-evaluated. A design project for cities scarred by the historical and political tragedy of war, such as Mostar and Beirut, will clearly not involve the same considerations as planning strategies for cities like Paris or Sydney. The difference lies in the lack of predictability in the post-war planning process, when it is almost impossible to foresee the future economical and political environment with continually shifting sectarian allegiances and volatile city administrations at work.

The social disintegration of many Western cities from Los Angeles to Johannesburg has led a number of authors to liken them to cities destroyed by war (Bollens, 1999; Lang, 1997; MacGinty, 2001). Certainly, many cities are characterized by high levels of residential segregation. While this division is essentially caused by economic and market forces and reflects differences in class, status and power, it has also resulted in racial, ethnic and religious divisions in many cases. Added to high levels of unemployment and poverty, racial and religious prejudice has led to tensions and rivalries that have spilt over into periodic rioting in many multi-ethnic and multi-faith cities in North American and Europe, such as in Paris in 2005.

Barakat (1998: 11–12) identifies three motivations for violent conflict in such cities:

- *Conflicts of a religious or ethnic nature.* The concept of 'cleansed' cities, promoted by ethnically motivated politicians, has resulted in separatism and the creation of mini-apartheid states within communities. Segregated neighbourhoods have been fostered where a rich multi-ethnic interaction (for example, Mostar, Sarajevo and Vukovar) formerly existed.

- *Conflicts of a civilian character.* Many cities have become increasingly targeted in today's conflicts, with once-cosmopolitan centres turning into battlefields as, for example, in Beirut, Mostar, Sarajevo, Banja Luka, Kigali and Kabul. These conflicts have been fed by a widespread proliferation of small arms, anti-personnel land-mines and 'second-hand' weaponry.

- *Conflicts between the 'haves' and 'have-nots'.* This urbanization of war is not just about ethnic division, it is also a war between the haves and have-nots and, in a number of cases such as Kabul and Sarajevo, it is about the long-ignored rural communities who, through violence, make a statement against the urban centres that have always received greater attention and better treatment.

However, Jerusalem is not Cleveland and, 'Beirut is not Pompeii', as Lebanese politician, Ghassan Tueni, remarked (Tueni, 1998: 292). The destruction caused by war and the subsequent erasure of civic memory in destroyed cities is critically different from that of the street violence of urban ghettos and riots. One fundamental difference is between the systematic and strategic destruction of significant monuments and prewar icons, such as Warsaw's historic centre, the Stari Most Bridge in Mostar and Beirut's former down-town district, and the physical manifestations of blight and neglect in many urban areas.

For example, the pervasive urban violence against Mostar was described as follows: 'Using every available weapon, the aggressor perpetrated a planned cultural genocide and urbicide systematically destroying all aspects of urban life, which symbolized our coexisting communities' (Association of Sarajevo Architects, 1989).

Another critical difference between cities destroyed by war and those undergoing social decay is in the operation of city management. While access to health, transport and infrastructure may become difficult in the micro-conflicts between the marginalized communities in cities such as New York, Amsterdam and Oslo, there is still a legitimate government and administrative structure in place to manage the situation. However, in macro-conflicts of the war-divided cities, the lack of legitimate authorities to administer basic city services only accentuates the problem. The fundamental differences between war destruction and urban decay are illustrated in Figure 1.5.

The continual state of siege from armed military and civilian conflict that cities such as Beirut, Sarajevo and Mostar suffered in their respective countries' civil wars created deep political and psychological trauma. Again, such trauma has often festered over decades of ethnic hostility and cannot always be equated with that resulting from the random urban violence of, say, the 2005 Paris and Sydney riots or the daily 'drive-by shootings' in poor, racially divided North American cities such as New Orleans, Detroit

Figure 1.5
WAR DESTRUCTION VERSUS URBAN DECAY

and Chicago. During a state of siege, the day-to-day eruptions of conflict in cities 'at war' also shut down the full operations and infrastructure of transport, telecommunications, health and civil services of any normal functioning city. While the experience of conflict-induced partition may have superficial similarities to the ethnic segregation of Paris and its *banlieux* and the ghettoization processes in North American cities, the latter are different in that people still have water, electricity and a functioning government in these (at least technically) 'non-war' zones.

This discussion of the manifestations of urban conflict is described in *City of Quartz* (1993), where urban geographer Mike Davis examines a series of contemporary urban walls created by the proliferation of violence in American cities such as Los Angeles and New York. In his extraordinary portrait of the underbelly of Los Angeles, Davis describes the militarization of urban space through the rise of gated residential communities in the USA and the divisive impact of infrastructure systems such as highways across major cities in the country. Davis's work is part of an emerging body of literature on the demise of North American, South American and European cities as peaceful and democratic entities. This reflects the proliferation of fortified enclaves and New Urbanist developments. The emergence of gated residential areas, guarded shopping malls and enclaves of office parks isolated from the central business district (from Johannesburg to Los Angeles) are in many respects a response to the perception of the city as an unsafe place by shutting out what Manuel Castells often terms 'structurally irrelevant people' (Castells, 1992). This social exclusion subsequently materializes in spaces that are privatized, enclosed and highly monitored for residential consumption, leisure and work.

Existing research

> In the libraries of schools of architecture and planning, the section for 'war and the city' continues to expand to include new titles but … [these] are often plans for buildings and infrastructures which, for no other reason than that they are sited in areas razed by war, are conveniently defined as 'reconstruction plans'.
>
> (Somma, 2002: 3)

Despite the emerging streams of research in the study of ethnicity, conflict and urbanity (Barakat, 2005; Bollens, 2000; Hasic, 2002a), to date there has been little systematic mapping of the relationship between sectarian conflict and design responses after war. While several authors have sought to engage with the issues of post-conflict emergency repair (Barakat, 2005; Yarwood, 1998), appropriate policy-making structures for war-damaged cities (Bollens, 1999), the rebuilding of particular cities and buildings destroyed by war (Diefendorf, 1990; 1993; Hasic, 2002b) and the historical backgrounds behind design decisions in cities such as Beirut and Nicosia (Hocknell, 2001; Sarkis and Rowe, 1998) there has been little comparative research informing design professionals about effective examples of using architecture as a peace-building tool.

Much historical and political data has been already gathered in a broad range of post-war cities, including the case studies of Beirut, Nicosia and Mostar. There has also been more recently a burgeoning post-9/11 body of criticism debating the highly vexed politics of how to rebuild the World Trade Center site.[7] In most cases, however, the issues surrounding post-disaster reconstruction are treated in a spatial manner and do not leave the reader with any road map on how to learn from the mistakes of past reconstruction efforts. That is, most recent commentators on post-war reconstruction, have mainly explored the social and cultural manifestations of war rather than the physical results of war and future spatial patterns of the city under scrutiny.

The divisions of war are also often naively characterized, as Calame and Charlesworth (2006: 6) suggest, as 'the by-product of irrational forces, such as traditional tribal hatreds or indelible social and religious attitudes that have been ingrained so deeply as to be insurmountable'. However, such views are not always an adequate response to the urban disintegration caused by war. Another problem with the state of this research field is the lack of comparative studies. While single case studies are valuable and, indeed, support the research undertaken for this book, comparisons across a range of post-war cities are needed to reach broader and surer conclusions and to develop relevant and coherent models for future urban policy and design frameworks for intervention.

Cities now being divided by ethnic conflict, such as Mitrovica in Kosovo and Basra in Iraq, continue to emerge as time goes on, while strong physical and psychological wounds still persist in cities such as Jerusalem and Belfast because of competing ethnic identities and territorial claims of sovereignty. All these pressures materialize in increasing demands for group rights and access to housing and infrastructure. However, there has been little architectural research or focused design effort seeking to address the specific problems of urban areas divided by sustained ethnic and religious conflict. The small field of academic research and practice in the field of cities destroyed by war tends to focus on the development of intelligent and well-argued but, ultimately, inapplicable urban policy principles. Other writers reveal the aesthetization and fetishization of war-destroyed cities as objects for obscure architectural strategies or quasi-philosophic urban meanderings on destruction, ruins and memory (see Bevan, 2006; Plunz, 1998; Woods, 1998).

The contributions of architects and other design professionals to the social reconciliation of war-divided cities have thus been marginal and their expertise is considered relevant only in the immediate emergency of repairing shelters and public hygiene infrastructures

and in the final implementation phases of reconstruction projects. Indeed, the critical political decisions and treaties[8] that have framed the reconciliation of partitioned societies
have rarely involved the professional input of architects. Given the proliferation of civilian
conflicts outlined earlier in this chapter, the task therefore in this study is to move
forward, beyond the academic rhetoric, with more practical recommendations for how
architects can engage directly and effectively in the peace-building and reconstruction
process following sustained urban conflict and destruction.

In summary, a number of key issues emerges from a review of the post-disaster reconstruction literature that inform subsequent chapters on case study and design studio
investigations:

- *The myth of the unitary city* which sees urban centres as coherent and democratic
  organisms. Cities that may appear healthy and successful can become the stage for
  protracted civil conflict. These urban centres also easily become the targeted playground for random (New York City) and sustained (Belfast) civil conflict.
  Recognition of patterns can assist in the development of professional effective
  responses to new scenarios of inter-ethnic urban violence.

- *The need for planners and architects to work within more interdisciplinary frameworks.*
  The underlying critique from many of the experts in the reconstruction profession
  (and through fieldwork to be examined in subsequent chapters) is the absence
  of implementing physical planning polices and projects within a wide category of
  professionally relevant disciplines such as sociology, psychology and environmental
  studies. Where such a strategy has been adopted, for example through the Nicosia
  master plan process, the tangible benefits of the planning process become much
  more obvious. The Beirut Master Plan project developed a 'scenarios approach' by
  a team of architects, planners, economists and sociologists looking at a number
  of different spatial trajectories for the currently divided city over a long-term
  period for a number of different users. In the absence of political reunification,
  such visions can give severed communities at least some hope for a future non-
  partitioned city.

- *The need to test architectural and planning theories through on the ground projects.*
  A key argument of this book is the need to develop a more complex understanding of the *causes* and possible *solutions* behind the post-war city scenario, through
  physically testing theoretical positions via architectural and landscape projects. This
  can be much more effective than simply devising abstract post-recovery 'wish lists'
  and one line planning 'mantras'. For example, a key outcome of undertaking workshops in the three case study cities of Beirut, Mostar and Nicosia, discussed in
  Chapter 8, was my re-examination of the popular urban design clichés and methods

address the persistent religious and socio-economic tensions still dividing the physical and mental terrain of Lebanese society.

Chapter 5 investigates the case study of Mostar. It analyses the massive exodus of local architects and the city's reliance on foreign design experts in its reconstruction programme, 1994–2004. This chapter explores the post-war city phenomenon through the theme of design as reconciliation. Reconciliation remains both a need and an obstacle between the still-polarized post-war Muslim, Serbian and Croatian communities resident in Mostar.

Chapter 6 focuses on a case study of Nicosia. It explores the role of architects and planners in envisioning an undivided Nicosia, through the planning mechanisms of the Nicosia master plan. I examine Nicosia through the theme, 'design as resolution' – resolution between the Greek and Turkish Cypriot groups still separated by the island's infamous Green Line.

In searching for common themes across the three case studies of Beirut, Nicosia and Mostar, Chapter 7 speculates how design professionals can actively contribute to the peace-building processes necessary in resolving the multiple physical and social effects of the post-war reconstruction scenario. That is, I examine how we may move from 'zones of contention' to 'lines of connection'. I compare the themes and patterns of reconstruction that have emerged from the three case studies and describe how architects have ignored (Beirut), tolerated (Mostar) and almost bridged (Nicosia) the pressing social and physical agendas of war-induced conflict. In this chapter, I also propose a flexible road map guided by three 'p' principles for built environment professionals navigating the complex environment of post-disaster zones.

Chapter 8 concludes with a summary of design studios undertaken in the case study cities and their implications for design educators. It suggests that new architectural tools are needed after sustained civil conflict, that disruptive urban conflict is not exclusive to formal 'war zones' and, finally, that there is a moral imperative for architects to contribute to the peace-building process after conflict.

Notes

1   Interview with Salma, Beirut, 8 June 2000.

2   Interview with Urban Planning lecturer, Queens University, Belfast, 9 August 2000.

3   These interviews were conducted with my colleague Jon Calame originally as field research for the 'Divided Cities Project' funded by the Macarthur Foundation in 1999.

4   Figures (courtesy of Jon Calame), taken from the *Armed Conflict Dataset*: Håvard Strand, Lars Wilhelmsen and Nils Petter Gleditsch; International Peace Research Institute, Oslo (PRIO), Version 1.2a, 14 March 2003.

5   Statistics on the human costs of war are abundant and contradictory. See Matthew White *Historical Atlas of the Twentieth Century* <http://users.erols.com/mwhite28/warstats.htm> was first placed online 18 October 1998 and last updated on 25 January 2003.

6   This included 11.7 million in UNHCR statistics and 3.7 million Palestinian refugees under the aegis of UNRWA. See Crisp, Talbot and Cipollone (2002).

7   See Ockman (2002), Sorkin and Zukin (2002), Vale and Campanella (2005) and Bevan (2006).

8   These include the 1998 Good Friday Agreement in Northern Ireland and the 1996 Dayton Plan, for Bosnia. For further details on Bosnia, see International Crisis Group report, *Is Dayton Failing?* (ICG, 1999).

9   'Trauma-glam' was a term used in 2001 by American University of Beirut academic, Richard Becherer, to describe the architectural propensity to glamorize the physical ruins of post-war cities like Beirut.

10 'Dystopia', the opposite of utopia, describes an 'imaginary place or state in which the condition of life is extremely bad, as from deprivation, oppression, or terror' (see <http://www.dictionary.com>).

11 Michel Foucault's 'heterotopias', are explained as 'places which are absolutely different from all sites that they reflect and speak about' (Foucault, 1986: 24).

12 For further details see Holden and Holford, 1951.

2

Architects and war

Figure 2.1
THE NEW JERUSALEM WALL

> *There has always been another war against architecture going on – the destruction*
> *of the cultural artifacts of an enemy people or nation as a means of dominating,*
> *terrorizing, dividing or eradicating it all together*

> *(Bevan, 2006: 8).*

War and architecture have a long and often parasitical relationship; the building and
unbuilding of urban centres, the making of enclaves, walls and segregated residential and
city zones have been fundamental to urban form and human experience. The destruction of buildings and cities has therefore always been an integral part of winning and
loosing wars.

In medieval cities like Vienna and Dubrovnik, external city walls provided freedom, privileges and protection for their inhabitants in city-states. In ancient China, armies demanded wide avenues between city blocks to ensure troop manoeuvrability and access. In 1989, the Tiananmen Square massacre in 1989 provided a potent metaphor for the reassertion of state control through the enforcement of violence on public space. More recently, the re-erection of yet another wall in Jerusalem, 25 feet high and part of a 21-mile barricade, is being built to separate Israelis and Palestinians (Figure 2.1).

A further example of urban violence relating to the history of urban reconstruction was when Baron Haussmann cut through the dense labyrinth of medieval Paris in the mid-nineteenth century to create a militarily accessible city. From the legally chartered Jewish ghettos in Venice and Warsaw from the fifteenth to the twentieth centuries, to the racially polarized townships under the former apartheid regime of South Africa, to the divided urban centres of Berlin and Jerusalem, cities have continually been broken, besieged and built again in the cause of reconstituting civil society. The three case studies, Beirut, Nicosia and Mostar, are therefore just a contemporary extension of a historical and spatial typology of civic discord and violence.

In view of this increasing spread of 'urbicide', that is, urban centres that have been destroyed by war and civil conflict, I explore the ways in which design professionals since 1945 have contributed to social stability after conflict. This is illustrated through historical and contemporary reconstruction case studies from France, Germany and the UK after 1945, to the role of designers in the 'post-9/11' era. Two central themes that are pivotal to any comparative analysis of post-war reconstruction are explored in this chapter. The first relates to the aesthetics of rebuilding: that is the question of whether the city should be reconstructed in the style it once was (as in the historicist rebuilding of Warsaw) or whether it should be reconstructed anew (as in the modernist rebuilding of Rotterdam). The second theme relates to those who are doing the reconstruction and what measures they have taken for public consultation. As a corollary, it is worth examining who among the general public is consulted in the rebuilding process – or whether the decisions are made entirely by the government or privatized rebuilding agencies (as in Beirut)?

Tabula Rasa versus Fascimile Cities

*Make sure not to ask yourself, has it got to be modern architecture or local
architecture, because those who ask this question demonstrate that they have not*

for a modern Germany were those that supported the increasing industrial and functionalist nature of its society. In his critique of modernist architecture, *Trouble in Utopia*, Robert Hughes notes the significance of this attitude among Bauhaus architects who believed: 'Re-educate the people and they will grasp the necessity – the moral necessity of a new form of shelter. Walter Gropius and Mies Van Der Rohe in Germany, no less than Le Corbusier in France, believed in the mirage of the architects as sociological priests' (Hughes, 1980: 167).

In a similar way, Adolf Hitler's rejection of modernist architecture was based upon the assumed connections between the social focus of architectural modernism and left-wing Bolshevik behaviour. As a result, the Nazis eventually closed the Bauhaus School in 1933, forcing many architects, including Walter Gropius, to flee to other countries. However, after 1945, there was a strong movement in Germany against the neoclassical architecture of Hitler's regime, most notably against the work of his chief architect and later Minister of Armaments, Albert Speer. Thus, the post-war reconstruction of German cities such as Dresden and Hamburg was based upon the concept of the 'zero hour' (*Stunde Null*), with the connotation of rebuilding as 'new beginnings with no past'. Fischer discusses how 'one moved from building directly to politics and morality with wholesale clearance on a nationwide scale as a means of rejuvenating social conduct and the national economy' (Fischer, 1990: 133). Fischer also argues that German architects, such as Gropius, thought that Germany could be used as a guinea pig to show what architects could do for the rest of Europe and the whole world.

However, despite this near-missionary fervour, much post-war architecture was reduced to the technical task of coping with the scale of the reconstruction and building required. For example Hans Adrian, Hanover's post-war chief city planner, stated that 'in the 15 years after the war, the goal was not to decorate Hanover or to build an attractive city, but to solve efficiently the housing problem' (cited in Diefendorf, 1993: 63). Architecture per se therefore often took a subordinate place where reconstruction was seen as a 'technical' rather than as an 'aesthetic' task, and many buildings reflected 'the rote application' of 'formulas by architects and contractors'. As a result, many critics spoke of architecture losing its way in the late 1940s with large tracts of cities becoming virtual no man's land.

In the UK, the planning of post-war reconstruction had begun, ironically, before the war had actually ended. The zeal to rebuild Britain immediately after the war has been described by Gordon Cherrey as a kind of 'social and spiritual renewal': planning of one kind had won the war and urban planning 'would win the peace' (Cherrey, 1990: 213). There was also a widespread belief that the Second World War would be 'the war to end all wars' that the First World War had failed to be. As a result, reconstruction planning was to be for good, rather than until the next war. Parallels were also made between the rebuilding of London in 1945 and the rebuilding of the city by Christopher Wren after the Great Fire in London in the seventeenth century. A congratulatory letter written to Wren in 1707 notes: 'However disastrous it (the fire) might be to the then inhabitants, it had proved infinitely beneficial to their prosperity; conducing vastly to the improvement and increase, as well as the riches and opulence, as of the splendour of this city.'[3]

After the Second World War, under the supervision of town planners Patrick Abercrombie and William Holford, and guided by reconstruction manuals such as the *Planning Ministry's Handbook on the Redevelopment of Central Areas*, plans were quickly made to reshape radically the form of Greater London. At this time, as evidenced by commentaries in the *Architects Journal*, architects were seen as critical resources in the rebuilding task. For example, one editor of that journal commented in 1940: 'Simultaneously, severe air raids may at any moment show that the skill and resourcefulness of building professions and local building firms as essential … as ambulance and fire services.'[4]

Affected by this reconstruction zeal, in 1947 the city of Coventry appointed a radical modernist architect, Donald Gibson, to review their overcrowded and vastly underplanned city. Gibson's task was to guide the reconstruction of Coventry following the severe damage caused by German bombing during 1940. Much of this reconstruction was guided by the first modern Town and Country Planning Act, which was established as a result of war damage in the UK. The Act, as Lewis shows, was intended 'to put back what had been destroyed and to make believe that the exigencies and privations of war to have been worthwhile – but not in order to make the impact and effects of another war less severe' (Lewis, 1989: 26).

Amazingly, in London, the Modern Architecture Group had produced a radical master plan for the city in 1939, well before bombs had actually targeted the city. This meant that when post-war reconstruction concepts were needed, there was already a template to work with. As Britain had experienced minimal political disruption during the war compared with Germany and France, it actually began exporting its reconstruction expertise to other war-devastated nations after 1945. For example, in 1947 a team of British Council-sponsored planners made lecture tours throughout Germany, focusing on prefabrication techniques in residential construction (Cherrey, 1990: 217).

Contemporary practice

As mentioned at the beginning of this chapter, the actions of contemporary architects, as we will see in Beirut, Nicosia and Mostar, have been much more limited in conviction and scope than in the aftermath of the Second World War. The current idea of 'relief-driven charitable actions' to freeze conflict appears to be the *modus operandi* of many professionals who were employed by international development agencies. This idea of post-war reconstruction as a charitable action (so that architects feel disempowered to act outside their relief mandate) is in stark contrast to the bold thinking by Second World War architects and planners, expressed in Le Corbusier's words, 'architecture or revolution!' This represented the view of many in the profession after 1945, who believed that they were empowered to make a difference to the welfare of civil society.

The notion that the architect has a social contribution to make in tackling the complex issues of the post-war chaos, such as ethnic polarization, has been problematic since the 1960s. This situation, the reasons for it, and the consequences are analysed in more detail in the following case study chapters. However, a new practice based upon the integration of social and physical reconstruction is emerging, even if it is not yet common. Seeking to build social capital and community capacity for local control of reconstruction, as we will see in Nicosia, this community-based approach envisaged architects working in interdisciplinary teams, consulting and engaging with residents in war-torn cities. This involved developing pilot projects to evaluate alternative design approaches and identifying appropriate processes for implementing reconstruction plans.

While architecture has not often played a major role in community-based reconstruction, other professions, including medicine and engineering, have developed strong programmes for working in post-war environments. For example, the mandate of Médecins Sans Frontières (MSF) is to work in countries where health structures are insufficient or even non-existent. Médecins Sans Frontières also works in remote health-care centres and slum areas, and trains local personnel. Engineers for Relief (RedR) has the similar goal of relieving suffering in disaster situations by providing competent and efficient personnel to humanitarian aid agencies worldwide. Engineers for Relief members provide front-line agencies with the technical assistance vital to restoring the everyday lives of affected communities, such as rebuilding roads and bridges, re-establishing fresh water supplies, managing waste, restoring communications and protecting the environment.

While architects have much to learn from the professions of medicine and engineering, two issues need to be taken into account. First, the skills of medical doctors and engineers are especially needed in the immediate post-crisis environments to treat the wounded and traumatized, refit hospitals and health centres, repair roofs and walls to make buildings habitable, and ensure vital services of water purification and waste-water treatment. Their skills are needed in the long term also. However, it seems to be only *after* immediate crises have been overcome and reconstruction planning begins that the skills of design professionals are sought. Unfortunately, this is the period when international aid and development funding is usually in decline and reconstruction has become the preserve of the newly established political elites and their business partners. As explained above, this often does not provide a positive atmosphere for more consultative community-based approaches to the rebuilding challenge.

The second issue concerns the problems that may be caused by the international aid community. While respect for local decision-making is becoming increasingly considered the prime factor in international assistance in all areas of relief work, many critics have expressed concern about the problems that have been created by more centralized top-down approaches that rely on external experts. Thus, Logan's case study of the reconstruction of Hanoi found that the most difficult problem across from the practice of 'bringing in foreign experts on whistle-stop tours' (Logan, 1996: 45).

Urbicide: the city as target

At the moment the town as a real concept simply does not exist; it reveals itself in time past as a recollection or a pathetic reminiscence, or in time future as an elusive and unrealistic projection.

(Association of Sarajevo Architects, 1989: 15)

Figure 2.4
URBICIDE: THE BOMBING OF BELGRADE, 1999

Why are cities such desirable targets for military attack and civil violence? Defensive sites such as hilltops, for example Montreal, and river islands, for example Paris, were often chosen as the location for cities. Maiwandi and Fontenot (2002: 41) argue that war has also 'influenced the design of the city'. They cite the examples of Chinese and medieval European cities where, with their small narrow, maze-like streets and fortifications, 'the city has been a catalyst onto which the imprint of the uncertain and violent history of conflict has left its trace' (2002: 41). However, cities became the major site of destruction and death in war only in the twentieth century, with the invention of long-range aerial bombing in the Second World War. This has involved a shift of warfare from battlefields and the high seas to the use of the city and civilian populations as strategic targets both through conflict in the city and directed at the city. As Barakat (1998: 11) observes, 'Today, wars are fought not in trenches and fields, but in living rooms, schools and supermarkets'.

Within this strategic and deliberate destruction of memory, many writers on the subject of war and architecture see the proliferation of civil conflict as signalling a nega-tion of civil relationships and identity. Thus, many architectural theorists such as Wigley (2002) and Daniel Liebskind describe the process of destroying iconic buildings, monu-ments and streetscapes as using 'nostalgia as a lethal weapon'. In this regard, Serbian philosopher Darko Tanaskovic (2000) also suggests that in war today, 'It is not enough to destroy biological life; you have to destroy memory as well'. Tanaskovic quotes several others who hold similar views. These include the celebrated Croatian archi-tect Bogdan Bogdanovich (a specialist in designing war memorials), who lamented the 'ritual massacre of cities', and New York cultural theorist Susan Sontag who described the 'homicide of memory' in the former Yugoslavia. 'Guernica is now our Vukovar,' she claimed. Similarly, one group of Bosnian architects has described the systematic process of Serbian violence upon urban areas in the former Yugoslavia as 'urbicide' and 'culturicide'.[5]

Generally, however, cities become centres of violence between opposing sectarian or ethnic groups only when one or more groups are frustrated by the lack of state redress of long-held perceptions (and reality) of injustice and repression. As Israeli urban planning academic Oren Yiftachel notes, inter-ethnic violence is rarely a factor in pluralistic societies where structures are in place to encourage immigrant groups to assimilate over time. In such societies, he states, 'One's ethnic affiliation is a private matter and ethnic movements mainly focus on the attainment of civil and economic equality' (Yiftachel, 1995: 218). However, ethnic conflicts are potentially explosive in those deeply divided societies composed of non-assimilated groups, which occupy their historical (real or mythical) homelands and where there is little state infrastruc-ture to redress discontent.

Cities, as home to the greatest numbers and diverse groupings of people in a country, are thus likely to be a source of unrest and any subsequent violence. Indeed, their civilian populations constitute what Bollens describes as 'soft, high-value' targets for larger unsettled conflicts. In explaining this concept, he states: 'Cities are fragile organisms subject to economic stagnation, demographic disintegration and cultural suppression' (Bollens 1999: 67). These pressures make cities particularly vulnerable, especially in situ-ations of asymmetrical conflict in which groups that lack resources or power can achieve a maximal disruptive impact from acts of aggression and violence. However, with the deliberate targeting of urban civilians, the goal of war has become not just the destruction of buildings and infrastructure, but also the destruction of culture.

The following chapter expands on the historical and contemporary roles for architects discussed in this section and proposes the development of a typology of six roles that architects may play in post-disaster cities. These *archetypes* illustrate the wide range of ways in which architectural capacities may be utilized in all stage of the post-conflict situation and set the scene for a comparative analysis in the subsequent reconstruction case studies of Beirut, Mostar and Nicosia.

Notes

1   See Sorkin and Zukin (2002), Ockman (2002) and Vale and Campanella (2005).

2   Extensive discussion of citizen participation after the Second World War in reconstruction in Germany and Poland is made in Diefendorf (1990; 1993) and Ciborowski (1956).

3   Quoted from *Report on the Reconstruction in the City of London* (1994) Report on the Preliminary Draft Proposals for Post-war Reconstruction in the City of London, B.T. Batsford.

4   *Architects Journal*, 23 May: 519, 1940.

5   See Hasic (2002b). These terms have been used frequently in describing the anti-city sentiments in the Bosnian conflict.

3

Archetypes

ROLE	METAPHOR	OUTCOMES
PATHOLOGISTS	Architects as physicians of space. City as body. Reconstruction as surgery.	Incremental master planning and radical urban 'surgery'
HEROS	Architects as messiahs, gods.	Architectural monuments, utopian cities and buildings as objects d'art.
HISTORICISTS	Architects as conservationists and nostalgists.	Cities in nineteenth century stasis (for example Berlin): the 'as it was, where it is' approach.
COLONIALISTS	Architects as imperialists.	Foreign visions implanted onto the urban form.
SOCIAL REFORMERS	Architects as peace builders and political actors within larger policy framework.	Design and planning as a public consultation to address social integration as well as physical rehabilitation problems.
EDUCATORS	Architects as curriculum reformers introducing community approaches to reconstruction into design studio process.	Raising architectural awareness in the next generation to effect change in post-conflict areas.

Figure 3.1
ARCHETYPES

This relationship between history, power and culture illuminates many of the problems that architecture then faced, and faces still.

(Wright, 1991: 13)

How can architects play more effective and varied roles in cities torn apart by ethnic and social conflict? While remaining conscious of the limits of architecture to determine social behaviour, the objectives of this comparative analysis of three post-war cities are, first, to outline design responses to the destruction and, secondly, to investigate whether specific typologies of effective design responses emerge through this investigation. A review of past, contemporary and potential future roles for architects in reconstruction allows the development of a range of what I call 'archetypes' – or prototypes of architects – in other words, roles that architects may play in post-conflict cities. These roles illustrate the wide range of ways in which design capacities may be utilized in all stages of the post-war reconstruction phase. They are described here in this chapter as they sketch out a framework for analysis, which is used in the three case studies. The key elements of the typology are summarized in Figure 3.1.

Architects as pathologists

The planner should be able to distinguish between sick spaces and spaces linked to mental and social health which are generators of the hearth. As a physician of space, he should have the capacity to conceive of a harmonious social space.

(Lefebvre, 1996: 152)

Architects as pathologists seek to diagnose the post-war city and prescribe the right medicine in the aftermath of sustained civil conflict. This role suits the post-war reconstruction goals of domestic peace, restructuring the economy and recapturing lost investment and tourist dollars. Lebanese writer Makdisi (1990), for example, has analysed the way Beirut's privatized planning agency, Solidere, presents itself as a healing agency, operating to help the city recover from its multiple afflictions. Using the same medical metaphor, Khalaf (1993: 42) argues that the Solidere process has sought to establish and monitor a stable heartbeat within the city without too much knowledge of the past trauma itself. He alleges that this situation has contributed to a collective post-war amnesia in Beirut, if not highly selective memory, and a 'continuing mood of lethargy, indifference and weariness'. Indeed, there are many types of selective memories ranging from nostalgia to denial, in cities after war.

These selective memories – a phenomenon common to most cities traumatized by war and repression – are not always easy to acknowledge or understand, precisely because the selectivity usually serves a political purpose: to justify the claims of one group over a competing group. The problem about the pathologist's role is that these medical conditions may persist after the 'surgery' of reconstruction if people are not involved in the planning and decision-making process. The role of the architect can be critical in this but, unfortunately, when acting as a pathologist, architects often miss valuable opportunities.

The architect as pathologist often takes on the role of the psychiatrist. For example, *The Berlin Wall Disease* (1973), which was written by prominent Berlin psychiatrist,

Dr Muller-Hegemann, Dietfried (1973) *Die Berliner Mauer-Krankheit* documented the ways in which East Berlin patients suffered from depression and other psychological ills owing to the closure of the Berlin border in 1961, The problems identified by Muller-Hegemann in East Berlin families included schizophrenic lives and the stresses and pressures of living in a constant, unrelenting state of surveillance, manifested by the erection of the wall. Similarly, the targeted destruction of cities in the Second World War is said to have had the geographical consequence of 'place annihilation', which left war survivors feeling 'their world had come to an end' (Hewitt, 1997: 296). The destruction of the city environment in post-war German cities, Hewitt (1997: 297) claims, 'left people's internal maps adrift, no longer fitting the space to which it had corresponded'. The diagnosis of *The Berlin Wall Disease* and Hewitt's concept of 'place annihilation' is a larger metaphor for the inescapable damage to socio-spatial relationships in a post-disaster city. Such relationships are critical in the conception of design projects for cities such as Beirut and Mostar, and are amenable to analysis and identification by physical planners early in the reconstruction process through genuine public consultation with local residents and relevant stakeholders.

While discussing architectural surgery, architects can also be seen as facilitators of control and order, and as curing pathological diseases by excising 'diseased cells'. Many architects interviewed for the Beirut case study, for example, described the eviction of low-income residents from the Elyssar residential project in Beirut as, 'cutting out the cancers' and architects as 'correcting the wrong cells' (Yayha, 2000). When the directors of the development project were asked why low-income residents were being displaced from the Elyssar construction site, the simple response was; 'C'est l'urbanisme de guerre – c'est la vie' (It is the urban planning of war – that's life) (Yayha, 2000).

Again in Lebanon, former Prime Minister Hariri discussed the 'heart–body'[1] metaphor of Beirut's reconstruction in suggesting that mending of the heart of Beirut – that is, its central business district – was critical to the functioning of the whole country – that is, its body. While medical analogies for architects are often convenient metaphors, Till suggests that, in fact, during the process of urban surgery, architects should be playing the part of the caring and supportive nurse, rather than the prescriptive, know-it-all doctor. He remarks that 'the actions of nurses are humanly conditioned, socially embedded but also remarkably tough' (Till, 1997: 111).

The correct and humane diagnosis of the reconstruction process, as related to the role of the architects in the post-war situation, is thus a critical but commonly over-looked one. In light of current accelerating global warfare discussed in Chapter 1, it could be suggested that inept post-war settlement reconstruction may provoke future terrorism. Equally, community-based reconstruction may be the most single important contribution towards its prevention.

Architects as heroes

Within this well-worn perspective, the architect perceives and imagines himself as an architect of the world, a human image of the god creator.

(Watson and Bridge, 1995: 67)

The contemporary concept of architect as hero results largely from the architectural celebrity ranking system operating within the international design community. In this elite hierarchy we see continual professional and press glorification of individual architects such as Frank Gehry, Rem Koolhaus, Daniel Liebskind and Peter Eisenmann. Till comments on the problematic celebrity role that many architectural educators promote: 'The idea of architect as artist plays an important part in establishing architectural culture to the outside world. It also affects the internal economy of the profession, with the "star architects" underpaying their staff, but offering an osmotic relationship with artistry in return' (Till, 1997: 109).

This hero, or Fountainhead[2] concept of architecture, while exciting fodder for glossy international design magazines and wealthy patrons, also creates the illusion of architecture as closed, finite and elitist. In recent times, the competition for rebuilding New York's World Trade Center has exposed the model of the architect as both a hero and a celebrity, dictating much of the public discourse about how to rebuild the site after the tragic events of 11 September 2001. It is ironic to note, as Wigley points out, that 'when the design of the twins was first revealed in 1964, the architect said they would be a manifestation of the relationship between world trade and world peace' (Wigley, 2002: 84).

After the World Trade Center disaster, many architects seemed all of a sudden to become experts in producing 'trauma-glam' architecture, as discussed in the introductory chapter. Some of New York's more 'signature' architects, Phillip Johnson, Peter Eisenmann, Bernard Tschumi and Cesar Pelli, as well as the foreign import, Berlin architect Daniel Liebskind, called for the immediate rebuilding of the towers. In this flagrant commercial post-9/11 environment, celebrity architects had their heyday in the local tabloid press. Sorkin comments about this design publicity-seeking, 'what has been added is a flaccid iconographic agenda and a grafted rhetoric of redemption and loss, so craven and self-serving as to make the skin creep' (Sorkin, 2003: 12).

Linked to the hero model is the supporting role of the architect as an independent artist and creative genius who refuses to sully his or her profession in any act of artistic compromise and has clear superiority over the rest of the construction team. This assigned heroism and artistry is much harder to achieve in the complex and fragmented political settings of broken cities such as Mostar and Beirut than in the glamorous urban metropolises of New York, Paris and London. Here, architects must often work within international development frameworks that demand broader socio-economic analysis rather than purely design-led solutions. In fact, the designer's role may often be extremely marginal, as the priorities are rebuilding infrastructure and basic health care. During the 1992–96 civil war in Mostar and Sarajevo, for example, the immediate repair of hospitals and basic water infrastructure for most local residents was seen as far more important than the repair of the Stari Most Bridge or the reconstruction of public buildings.

In Beirut, 'Jacques', a French architect who has worked in Beirut since 1965, commented that architects lack the ability to work outside this traditional mode of professional heroism: 'I think architects are not inclined to do the social work. They want to construct. The architect's education doesn't emphasize the public welfare. So few architects have this desire and if they have it, no one asks them to express it and if they end up doing it, no one listens!'[3]

In many ways, the idea of architect as hero also stems from the emphasis placed on the design studio component in architectural education. In the studio format, original-ity and one-upmanship is praised far more highly in the design process than, say, archi-tectural sustainability or the project's relevance to the client for whom the design project was originally conceived.

Supporting the hero concept of architecture is the exclusion of anybody who does not fit into the standard Western profile for the profession; that is, the 'stereotype of the heroic architect – white, male, middle-aged and moneyed' (Dyckhoff, 2003: 18). Despite the large numbers of women graduating with design degrees, architecture is still in fact a predominantly male domain and a 'closed clubby world' guided by 'endemic racism and sexism'. The hero model can be redeemed, however, if aesthetic concerns are merged with issues of social justice. There is, in fact, a group of architects already practising aesthetically compelling architecture that has a social purpose. Prime examples include Shigeru Ban's housing for victims of the Kobe earthquake and Samuel Mockbee's work for homeless communities in the USA. Mockbee's concept of the 'citizen architect' is relevant here when he suggests 'the practice of architecture not only requires the active participation in the profession, but it also requires civic engagement' (Bell, 2004: 155).

Architects as historicists

Everything's selective. I am not against being selective. I am against how to select. And I don't think normally you have to adore memory. Memory is selective of course, but who's selecting and how to select. This is the problem.[4]

Contemporary design approaches in most war-torn cities suggest that the reconstruction of historic city areas and cultural monuments are accorded top priority in the scheduling of the physical recovery process. For example, the rebuilding of Beirut's downtown district has focused solely on rebuilding of the former city centre and its associated archaeological relics, rather than embracing plans for the larger Beirut metropolis. Samir Khalaf (1993: 34) raises the same concerns of authenticity in the reconstruction process in his city, Beirut: 'How much of the ugly vestiges of war can or should be incorporated into the rebuilt fabric of Beirut? How much, in other words, should the new city look like the one which was destroyed?'

In this quest for historic authenticity, the peripheral scarred areas and dividing lines of the post-war city such as the Boulevard in Mostar and the Green Line in Beirut are commonly neglected areas. 'Amir' comments on the irony of rushing to rebuild the Stari Most Bridge in Mostar, when there was still little industry or associated employment for remaining Mostarians in the city:

> With this city of Mostar, because there is no reconstruction of factories, reconstruction of industry, we are reconstructing something more emotional, you know, like the bridge. What is [a] bridge? This is an emotional, political case but, like, the building [the bridge] is [a] piece of cake. They built it [the bridge] in the sixteenth century in five minutes. We are building some architectural elements, you know, but this is, like, not important![5]

However, since the Wall fell in 1989, it is, perhaps, Berlin that has represented the ultimate 'laboratory' for a discussion of architectural historicism. A battle of nostalgia, historicism and modernity has guided Berlin's chief city planner, Hans Stimmann, in rebuilding the city, in a style he labels 'critical reconstruction'.[6] This reification of the past in the (re)construction that has followed the reunification of Berlin has produced mixed results in a diversity of architectural styles by a wide range of international architects selected to work in re-envisioning the new German capital city.

Architects as colonialists

> The politicized climate of the colonies makes it clear that virtually any stylistic trend or policy reform can be used for political purposes. The possible implications of 'traditional' or 'modern' styles, of innovative or conservative policies, all come more sharply into focus.
>
> (Wright, 1991: 12)

Architects in cities such as Beirut, Nicosia, Mostar and Jerusalem are often working within a colonial mentality and framework, with an attitude that 'We know what is good for you'. This imperialist attitude is clearly not limited to post-war cities. Architectural theorist, Anthony King (1990: 146), comments, 'It was thought that modernism would save cities from Europe's industrialist-capitalist urban chaos'. Similarly, Sophie Watson and Gibson (1995: 8) describes the situation in South Africa, where 'The challenge is to overcome the fragmentation wrought by colonialism and modern planning', and in India, where 'the fragmentation exacerbated by British colonialism' must be overcome.

The tradition of architectural colonialists in this century has clearly been more success-ful at the scale of the object rather than an urban scale. For example, the modernist proj-ects of Chandigarh and Brasilia by Swiss architect Le Corbusier and his disciple, Oscar Niemeyer, respectively, are great architectural achievements, if you look at architecture as sculpture, but not in terms of the people for whom the architectural vision was made. In Israel, Oren Yiftachel (1995: 216) confronts 'the dark side of modernist planning' in an essay on Israeli minorities in Galilee, where he highlights the ways in which urban and regional planning has been used as an effective and insidious form of social control in many post-disaster societies.

The reliance on international aid agencies in countries such as Bosnia also protracts such colonialist–colonized relationships (Anderson, 1998; Yarwood, 1998). In Mostar, for example, architects have played only a small role in determining the future of their city, as they are completely dependent on foreign aid for reconstruction projects. 'Assem', a Lebanese architect discusses the perceived problems of outsider architectural experts arriving in Beirut to reconfigure his city: 'Who is going to recreate this fabric? People from Saudi Arabia? Bankers from AMRO bank? What's the destination and what class of society also [is it for]? It's going to be a paradise for the rich where you could enter it with a classic car and a gate.'[7]

However, 'Eric', a French urban planner in Beirut, sharply rejects the notion of foreign architects as colonialists: 'Colonialist, it is so caricatured! Now, when the Lebanese government has French people for their expertise it is also because there is no kind of quality, there are no urban planning specialists here. All the people who say, 'I am the specialist' are not good'.[8]

The tendency of architects to work in the colonialist mode can be linked to the standard curriculum in many architectural degrees where the traditions and norms of Western architecture and planning are seen as the benchmark for many young aspiring design-ers. For example, during my time teaching architecture in Beirut, from 2000 to 2002, there were no courses dealing with contemporary architecture in the Middle East. It was as if fashionable architects from New York and Paris had far more to teach young Lebanese architects than their neighbours and professional colleagues from Amman, Cairo or, more importantly, their own city, Beirut.

Architects as social reformers

Why are we here? This is a fundamental question and we need to do some soul searching. Are we here out of conviction, out of duty, or out of philanthropy for the less privileged of our fellow human beings?

(Khalaf, 1993: 24)

If the division lines of war are political, do architects have a political role within the broader mission of achieving social reform? Contemporary positions in the debate on architecture's socio-political role fall between a view of architecture as an instrument of capitalist production and a view of it as a transformative (and potentially manipulative) tool of social behaviour. In regard to the potential of architecture and planning as socially transformative tools, Jerusalem planner and politician, Meron Benvenisti expresses his pessimism about the profession's peace-broking capacities. He suggests that the efforts of most planners in the arena of inter-ethnic conflict are 'ineffective because of the complex relationship between "real" and "perceived" environments' (Benvenisti, 1982: 89).

As individuals, many architects may be concerned about issues of social and economic justice. Yet, over the past twenty years, the architectural profession has moved steadily away from engagement with complex and increasing civil conflicts and associated urban violence, or even such basic problems as homelessness, the degradation of urban environmental quality and the planning challenges posed by the rapidly changing demographic patterns of inner city migration. However, the capacity of architects to influence political process as social reformers does depend on the socio-cultural and legislative contexts in which they are operating. For example, architects can have substantially more impact in cities such as Paris and Barcelona, where there is a democratic planning framework, than they can in Beirut and Mostar, where this is clearly lacking. Local and international factors in Beirut can shape random segments of the new business central district. However, real-estate entrepreneurs there determine the city's planning framework, or lack of it, with little regard for the values of 'social democracy'[9] as in planning the Bercy social housing project in Paris. In Berlin, the role of architects as social reformers has been very limited, with a much greater concentration upon architecture as a corporate showcase via the inner-city Potsdamer Platz development. This well-publicized project created an architecturally sophisticated, but inevitably uninspiring, mega-urban shopping mall.

While a series of *grands projets* and macro-infrastructure strategies were developed by the Berlin 'post-Wall' planning administration, their lack of attention to the social and economic disparities between East and West Berlin communities prompts many Berlin architects nowadays to question the success of the city's reconstruction programme. For example, local architectural historian, 'Dieter' comments:

> There was a great confusion because of the two administrations and there was a necessity to merge them. And where there could be only one administration what happened is that the administration of the West absorbed the administration of the East because the administration of the West was much bigger and the West was winning in a way. It was a cruel process and it could not be a process of justice.[10]

In his seminal essay, 'Space, knowledge and power', Michel Foucault engages in this broader debate on the social role of architects: 'Architecture in itself cannot resolve social problems: I think that it can and does provide positive effects when the liberating intentions of the architect coincide with the real practice of people in the exercise of their freedom' (Rabinow, 1997: 36). Rather, Foucault argues that the city is a place of resistance and contestation, increasingly producing spaces of profound economic and ethnic exclusion. Writing in Paris during the 1960s at the same time as Foucault, Henri Lefebvre was concerned about the lack of social analysis in the field of urbanism and architecture. He comments: 'The right to the city manifests itself as a superior form of rights; right to freedom, to individualization in socialization, to habitat and to inhabit was not so much the home but the city that expressed and symbolized a person's complete being and spiritual consciousness' (Lefebvre, 1996: 67).

Unlike many of the complex writings of fellow French philosophers of his day (for example, Jean Paul Sartre, Merleau-Ponty and Simone de Beauvoir), Lefebvre was able to move from abstract musings on the city to a critical analysis of concrete examples of urban change and conflict in Paris, such as the destruction and subsequent renovation of the Les Halles district in central Paris in the early 1970s. Lefebvre's provocative discourse on architecture focuses on the increasing awareness in post-war Europe of the destruction and physical violation of cities via proliferating capitalist developments in and around many historic city centres.[11] His concept of a 'right to the city' emerged from an increasing awareness of the need for civil rights in the city for marginalized groups such as old people and women: 'The right to the city has become more essential than ever, it emerges as the highest form of rights: liberty, individualization in socialization, environs (habitat) and ways of living' (Lefebvre, 1996: 45).

The essential value of Lefebvre's work consists in provoking architects to be politically active in legitimizing citizen rights against exclusion from their city and its production, and in attaining a truly civil society. In this way, architects take on the role of public intellectuals, engaging with critical urban issues by writing and voicing opinions about the possible impacts of political decisions on city form. This is a role that Edward Said described as vital for anyone working in the public domain: 'The central fact for me is, I think, that the intellectual is an individual endowed with a faculty for representing, embodying, articulating a message, a view, an attitude, philosophy or opinion to, as well as for a public' (Said, 1994: 11).

Indeed, architectural and landscape projects can be used to bring conflicting parties to the table in the political mediation process. There is something tangible about an architectural plan as a basis for negotiation rather than just a series of discussions, policies or peace treaties. Using the tools of planning, that is, design workshops and long-term master plans, to reconnect post-disaster communities, again entirely depends on who is taking command of urban planning operations after the cessation of conflict. No other reconstruction episode illustrates more clearly this close and inseparable link between architecture and politics than Berlin's post-Wall rebuilding decade (1989–99). The most effective component of Berlin's rebuilding programme was the public participation process initiated under the 'Stadtforum'[12] (city forum) debates. The Stadtforums were public forums conducted after the fall of the Berlin Wall in 1989 through a process using questions and answers. These forums involved architects, politicians and resident groups commenting upon major development projects such as the Potsdamer Platz site. Gerald Bloomeyer, a Berlin architect, comments about the cathartic role of the Stadtforum series:

> I believe in dialogue. The major division is in our heads. At the end of the GDR, the Mayors of East and West Berlin asked us to put on a workshop with the best local and international planners. The results were discussed at an international conference for 500 people. This allowed many groups to meet for the first time. It was important to hear the different priorities politicians, investors and planners had.[13]

Architects should therefore be encouraged to adapt an advocacy role, as in the Stadtforums, to challenge dominant power structures, where needed, and to move beyond their usual activity as designers of mere 'objects' to engage in political action that affects both the spatial and social fabric of our cities. The idea of activism is clearly not new for the profession. Four decades ago, many architects and design academics were inclined to believe that political advocacy was essential to their practice. For example, in the 1970s Columbia University's architecture faculty, Avery Hall, was the centre of protests against the Vietnam War. In Paris in 1968, the École des Beaux Arts was one of the European centres of radical activity. In comparison, in the new millennium, there has been virtual silence from the architecture community on issues of profound change to the built environment, from the Kyoto Protocol to the new wall now being erected to divide Palestinians and Israelis.

Figure 3.2
THE DESIGN EDUCATOR

Architects as educators

Architectural educators can influence their students to think beyond the typical aesthetic concerns of most architectural education. As Till suggests: 'many schools of design are still guided by current obsessions with technological determinism, aesthetic formalism and theoretical obfuscation' (Till, 1997: 78). The world is replete with destroyed sites, either natural disaster or war induced, for academic investigation. Giving design students who have never encountered issues of urban violence and destruction the opportunity to work on sites of devastation can vastly increase their perception of their capability as future architects. According to a 1996 report by the Carnegie Foundation, 22 per cent of students enrolled in architecture school went into architecture to help improve the community: 'Many of these graduates find that they have to leave the traditional path of architecture if they want to fulfill this goal' (Scott-Ball, 2004: 132).

Foreign architectural students on summer school programmes can also be influential actors in the post-war rebuilding process by offering visions, hopes and possibilities while working with local architects and planners. Unfortunately, they can also see such sites as a laboratory for architectural exercises in what I label as 'trauma-glam' architecture, that is, form-making, with the ruins of the post-war city as merely a seductive backdrop. Mostar, for example, has experienced a great deal of architectural experimentation, such as the Columbia University 'New Urbanism's' studio in 1998 (see Plunz, 1998). While interesting in its 'deconstructivist' approach to the ruins of the city, this project failed to address any of the real housing, infrastructure and public space issues in the city.

In Beirut, many architects interviewed in the fieldwork phase of this book discussed this lack of integration between the reconstruction process and architectural education. 'George', an architect in Beirut, comments:

> And this is becoming a very difficult thing to do here [Beirut] because of the lack of debate in architecture. There are no awards, no competitions, no interesting

models to compete with, and no interesting intellectual positions to agree or disagree with; therefore architecture is not part of the cultural debate.[14]

Architectural education thus tends to have two critical voids. The first stems from the foundation curriculum where design is based upon precedent, that is, individual hero architects and their signature buildings. Here, the emphasis on the individual artist replaces the values of innovation, technical precision, moral rigour and social justice that are commonly emphasized in disciplines such as law, medicine and science. The biosciences have generated the new discipline of bioethics, and perhaps there is a need for a discipline of archi-ethics. Thus, architects commonly remove themselves from their profession's potential contribution to civil society if one assumes, as Andy Merrifield suggests, 'the ideal of social justice is the bedrock of any democratic society' (Merrifield, 1997: 1).

The second void rests in the lack of interdisciplinary-based teaching. Architecture is seen as a solo act, which has little or nothing to learn from other major fields, such as sociology, science, philosophy, law or medicine. As Till (1997: 107) remarks: 'The initial model on which the profession of architecture was founded is no longer flexible enough to cope with the changing conditions in society.' The current practice of archi-tectural education is therefore based on many stereotyped categorizations, buildings as art, architects as celebrities and design leading to enormous profits. Such a limited view of architectural education, in fact, frames many of the degree courses in design across Australia, Europe, the UK and the USA. A recent reflection by Dorrell (2003: 29) on the threatened closure of Cambridge University's well-regarded diploma programme in architecture also suggests the perceived lack of market relevance of the programme: 'The [threatened] closure will serve as a wake-up call to other universities. If Cambridge can no longer afford a department, then the clock must surely be ticking elsewhere.'

Lebbeus Woods is one of the few architectural educators who devote their practice and theoretical speculations to architecture in crisis and the condition of architecture on the edge. Woods (1997) has made a number of design propositions for Sarajevo.

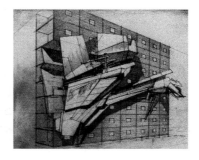

Figure 3.3
LEBBEUS WOODS: 'SARAJEVO APARTMENT PROJECT'

However, he rejects in his work the simulation of the prewar city as a style and he refuses to produce buildings that are designed to draw the admiration of tourists. Woods introduces us to a new post-war vocabulary of architecture and methods. His terms, almost like those of a medical anthropologist, include the scab, the scar ('to accept the scar is to accept existence') and finally the 'injection' of a building, 'filling in' the debris of the post-war landscape.

While his speculations and compelling vocabulary initially challenge us to look at the design of post-conflict space in new ways, Woods ultimately aestheticizes the post-war 'problem' into a kind of 'Ivy League' charette session. His 'spic and span' clinical renderings of new ruins sanitize war damage into some kind of post-holocaust theme park, leaving us with no real capacity or tools to actually mobilize any design solutions for the destroyed landscapes at hand.

Summary

Unlike our colleagues immediately after the Second World War, many contemporary design professionals are still not adequately prepared to take on the challenges of increasingly fractured urban centres, which clearly necessitate a radical revision of orthodox planning and architectural teaching methods. The academic career of most design students is still confined and dominated by the values and aspirations of corporate clients and celebrity professionals, rather than by the pressing social agendas of huge demographic urban change and endemic poverty in First and Third World cities. Worthington's (2000) suggestion of refocusing architectural education on the four principles of problem-solving, concept-defining, solution-framing and creating meaning provides a much more useful framework to broaden the scope for young architects and educators wishing to expand their future design careers by working on projects with a strong social and ethical context beyond the creation of merely individual objects.

Working and researching in post-war cities over the past decade (1994–2005), particularly in Mostar and Beirut, I have observed that many of these cities are critically under-resourced in the area of skilled design professionals willing to contribute to the peace-building processes necessary to establish normality. Too often, in the aftermath of conflict, the decision to intervene with design projects is based on the assumption that a stable democratic state is already in place. Political and economic uncertainties in post-conflict times are, however, constant undercurrents that design professionals must respond and adjust to in reconstruction planning. Waiting for so-called complete or final peace in order to act effectively can be too late, as we now see in the delayed reconstruction attempts in Afghanistan and Iraq, where many international aid agencies have deferred their rebuilding work until full co-operation has been established with local planning agencies.

Consequently, I propose that the problem-solving processes inherent in architectural conceptualization and production can also contribute to coping with the complexity of the reconstruction process. In a similar way, Lebanese architect Hashim Sarkis vows:

> I shall faithfully comply with my professional bias and show how spatial restructuring can inspire, rather than merely illustrate, social and political reconstruction. My larger agenda is to suggest the effective role that architecture might play in the re-structuring of Lebanese society and how this role can assist in the avoidance of reversion to disintegration.

> (Sarkis, 1993: 104)

Architects who forfeit such professional responsibility can become accomplices in maintaining division across polarized cities by ignoring the root causes of the social devastation (wrought by the conflict) and working for clients whose main concern is icon-building and speedy economic reconstruction at the expense of social reintegration and peace-making. They thus remain aloof from constructive decision-making processes related to urban growth, transition and long-term recovery in high-risk areas. For example, some designers I know working for the Solidere reconstruction project in Beirut have never visited the Palestinian refugee camps of Sabra and Chatila, only 2 kilometres from their downtown Centre Ville project.

A series of interviews in Beirut, Nicosia and Mostar between 1999 and 2001 revealed that the opinions of design professionals on the capacity of architects to contribute to post-conflict vulnerabilities often diverge. For example, 'Gus', a planner in Beirut comments:

> Probably you're asking too much of architects. I mean, my experience, of course, is that although architects present themselves as being people who understand best how cities work, they're generally not. I think you're asking a bit too much from architects to have a very deep response. It's a very complex situation.

'Amir' from Mostar, in contrast, suggests:

> An architect or a planner has a critical role to organize – to help the organization of life. If you put a bridge on a wrong place, it's a disaster. If you forget some bridge or put an entrance in a wrong place, you have a bad city and a sad community.

As discussed in Chapter 2, since the Second World War the role of architects in the reconstruction of war-damaged cities has become extremely marginal and their expertise has been seen as relevant only in the emergency phases of rebuilding projects. The critical political decisions and treaties leading to the reconciliation of polarized societies still rarely involve architects and planners. For example, neither the Dayton Peace Plan in Bosnia nor the Northern Ireland Good Friday Agreement (1998) mention anything about removing the physical partitions between feuding residential enclaves, either now or at any time in the future.

Contemporary architects working on the rebuilding of war-damaged cities have an ambiguous role. Is their mandate to act as social reformers or pathologists? Or should they confine their expertise to more aesthetic issues of heroic post-war architectonics? As mentioned earlier, the challenge within the reconstruction field lies in redefining new roles for architects as mediators and urban peace-builders, and as social reformers and educators. How practically then, as architects and planners, can we engage with, or mediate, political power in the post-partition chaos through the formulation of planning policies and architectural projects? This chapter has begun to propose a potentially more liberating, and perhaps more effective, future for architects, to work outside of traditional sites and methods of producing architecture. However, the case studies in the next three chapters reveal that the key word here is 'potentially'.

Notes

1   Interview with Rafiq Hariri, late Prime Minister of Lebanon, June 2000, Beirut.

2   *The Fountainhead* is a movie made in 1949 (starring Gary Cooper), based on a book by Ayn Rand about a heroic architect, Howard Roark.

3   Interview, Jacques, architect, August 2001, Beirut.

4   Interview, Elias, journalist, June 2000, Beirut.

5   Interview, Amir, architect, July 2000, Mostar.

6   See Wise (1998).

7   Interview, Assem, architect, June 2000, Beirut.

8   Interview, Eric, urban planner, October 2001, Beirut.

9   Based on an interview with Dominique Perrault, architect with APUR (Atelier Parisien D'Urbanisme), Paris, March 1999.

10   Interview with Dieter, historian, May 2000, Berlin.

11   Lefebvre practised what he preached in many respects, taking part in many inter-disciplinary projects with architects and planners, including the Galieni renewal

project in the north of Paris and that of the new city for Belgrade project in Yugoslavia in the early 1980s.

12   'Stadtforum Berlin' (city debates) was set up in 1990 as an informal planning tool of the Berlin Senate administration. Stadtforum's bi-monthly events are comple-mented by public discussions in the context of the series 'StadtProjekte', planning workshops on specific locations.

13   E-mail from Gerald Bloomeyer, Berlin architect, 10 September 1999.

14   Interview, George, architect, Beirut, July 2001.

4

Beirut – city as heart versus city as spine

This monster of a city, or city-region, is united in form, but pregnant with contradictions. It is marked with the scars of successive wars, visible in its diversified and inconsistent frontiers.

(Tueni, 1998: 285)

After sixteen years of brutal civil war (1975–90), Lebanon's capital, Beirut, is being rebuilt. This chapter focuses on the city's reconstruction by the private company Solidere and the implications for design professionals in the country. In analysing the rebuilding of Beirut, I examine the multiple causes of the city's physical destruction[1] and the problematic role of architects in the reconfiguration of the partitioned city. In doing so, it is necessary to question why many of the reconstruction plans currently being implemented fail to address the persistent religious and socioeconomic tensions still dividing the physical, intellectual, ethnic and emotional terrain of Lebanese society. The experiences of reconstruction in Beirut are an index of the professional issues and dilemmas faced by architects in other war-decimated cities. These include reliance upon foreign 'experts', a focus on physical infrastructure and *grands projets*, often with a heritage emphasis, and a systemic lack of engagement with local actors in the reconstruction process.

The fundamental problem with Beirut's rebuilding process lies in the durability and seductiveness of the metaphor of 'city as heart' (Charlesworth, 2004): the idea that

Figure 4.1
DOWNTOWN BEIRUT, 1995

the city can be revived through major 'surgery', namely, high-end, large-scale commercial and residential projects in the city centre where the architect performs his pathologist role. This metaphor has been perpetuated through the reduction of Lebanon's post-war reconstruction to rebuilding only a sliver of its capital city and reducing this in turn to the downtown *Centre Ville* project under the leadership of the now-deceased businessman and ex-Prime Minister of Lebanon, Rafiq al-Hariri. Hariri was assassinated in central Beirut on 14 February 2005.

Urban paradox

Beirut's rebuilding process has been bedevilled by contradictory accusations that it is 'self-inflicted destruction' versus claims that the reconstruction is an inner-city renaissance, with Hariri as a messiah and the private reconstruction agency, Solidere,[2] as his medium. Claims that Beirut is the world's largest laboratory for post-war reconstruction have been marketed through the metaphor of rebuilding the city's heart, as a way of validating the 'urban surgery' being performed. This surgery was intended to create what Saskia Sassen (1999) has described as a 'Glamour Zone' – the idea that global centres need to continually operate in a cutting-edge property market. However, this highly promotional focus on reconstructing the centre as the metaphorical heart of a destroyed city-body through privatized fast-track development strategies has led to an over-planned central urban area and a vastly under-planned greater Beirut metropolis.

The reconstruction of Beirut is undeniably a potent national symbol. Nevertheless the Solidere project affects only 1.8 square kilometres, approximately one-tenth of the destroyed city area, while little attention has been paid to the wider metropolitan region in formulating planning strategies for the post-war city of Beirut. Thus, schemes such as the *Centre Ville* project continue to produce segregated enclaves, serving only to remind the Lebanese even further of the immense and accelerating void between rich and poor in their country today. They are accompanied by a policy of laissez-faire governance in accordance with the US, International Monetary Fund (IMF) and World Bank requirements and subsequent Gulf investments, none of which does much to reduce the gap between rich and poor.

The role of architects in Lebanon's revival may be seen to have contributed to the physical and economic isolation of the rebuilding projects. Prompted by the urgency to put Beirut back on the international trade and tourism map, there has also been an assumption that a traditional, centralized master plan managed by a privatized development agency (Solidere) is an appropriate response to extensive national trauma. We may, however, learn from the errors of this strategy. My examination of Beirut as the primary case study in this investigation of post-war cities, therefore, focuses upon learning from the problems created by reducing post-conflict reconstruction to a real-estate development strategy with only minimal social accountability. By probing the successes and failures of the Beirut reconstruction model we may derive lessons applicable to other urban centres disrupted and destroyed by civil war and social conflict.

Two major design concepts guide existing and potential architectural and interventions in Beirut and are exemplified in the subsequent case studies of Mostar and Nicosia. These concepts are examined through an analysis of the historical suite of reconstruction projects that caused the rebuilding of post-war Beirut to be conceived as a speculative real estate project. These planning ideologies can be summarized as:

1   *City as heart*: the 'city as heart' vision sees the city as one large self-contained development field for real-estate speculation – based upon the argument that the focus on reconstruction should be the centre as the metaphorical heart of a destroyed city-body. This concept avoids one of the key problems of Beirut's reconstruction by excluding the demarcation line and the periphery of war-torn Beirut from rebuilding strategies and the absence of any comprehensive or metropolitan vision for the city's surrounding region.

2   *City as spine*: the 'city as spine' vision views the city as a dynamic and democratic entity. Reconstruction is therefore seen as a longer, sequential process based upon the gradual implementation of a number of small regeneration projects that, in time, repair and strengthen the social and physical 'backbone' of both the city and its many communities.

My research in Beirut was undertaken while living and working in Beirut between February 2000 and June 2002. Prior to living and working in Lebanon, my research and professional architectural experience in the post-war field had been based upon short visits, seven to ten days long, to a series of post-war sites from Beirut, Belfast and Nicosia to Berlin. Upon reflection, I realize that I often arrived armed with colonialist clichés in cities such as Beirut and Mostar, assuming that, for example, a master plan would be the right tool for bringing all conflicting parties to the table. The task of obtaining objective information on the rebuilding scenario also proved virtually impossible in Lebanon. For example, listening to colleagues involved in the Solidere project, I assumed that the whole reconstruction story in Beirut was a rather clever strategy of leveraging public capital and support to rebuild the devastated town.

My early opinions of Beirut's reconstruction were based mainly on the writings of authors such as sociologist Samir Khalaf (1993) and local architect Oussama Kabbani (1992). While these accounts were valid, they clearly privileged a middle-class and often biased political reading of the multiple economic difficulties experienced by most Beirutis who were unable to enjoy the fruits of the reconstruction process. Without the experience of living day-to-day with the multiple and conflicting contradictions of Beiruti culture, history and society, the challenge of understanding the city's destruction and more recent reconstruction would have been much harder.

In building a picture for determining the role of architects in the Beirut reconstruction process, interviews were undertaken with key actors such as politicians, architects, planners, residents, taxi drivers and journalists. The interviews ranged from official discussions with senior planners and the Prime Minister to impromptu interviews with residents and taxi drivers who still refused to 'cross to the other side' of the city's Green Line divide. Having been assured of confidentiality in the interview process, very few participants refused to allow our discussion to be formally recorded. Often the process of the interview itself felt like a catharsis for interviewees, as if no one else has been listening to their story, or nobody had even bothered to ask.

The cycle of destruction and reconstruction

> One of the most profound consequences of the war has been the redrawing of
> Lebanon's social geography, the most rudimentary social ties which normally cement
> a society together — ties of trust, loyalty, compassion, decency — which have been in
> many respects, grievously eroded. It is easier to recreate a state than to reassemble
> a society.
>
> (Khalaf, 1993: 17)

Beirut's reconstruction needs to be seen within broader historical cycles of destruction and reconstruction and the subsequent rebuilding and re-mapping of political and sectarian boundaries. To examine current planning strategies for Lebanon's capital city, the sequence of invasions, appropriations by colonial powers, and a history of planning failures and projects in the city should be understood. How, in fact, do these complex historical and social overlays lead to the government in Lebanon taking the role largely of a passive bystander rather than being an active participant in the spatial and social reconfiguration of the city's post-war reconstruction?

The Lebanese commonly refer to the civil war as *Al-Hawadeth*, an Arabic phrase suggesting not so much a war 'between each other' but a war of 'others'[3] on Lebanese soil. *Al-Hawadeth* literally means 'the events'. The use of this phrase represents a combination of denial (either of reality and/or responsibility) and the fact that the Lebanese were 'in it' [the war], but at the same time felt it was beyond their control. Thus many Lebanese people see themselves simultaneously as both witnesses and victims of 'the events'. It is also significant that many foreign accounts of the civil war allude to the Lebanese 'events' (Fisk, 1990; Khalaf, 1993; Sarkis and Rowe, 1998) and insist that the family/kin/clan (primary ties) remained the more powerful connectors during the war and after. Indeed, the government itself reflected not only religious sectarianism but also remnants of feudal patron – client relationships.

These 'events', assembled as 'the Lebanese civil war' were a series of events that were localized in region, in time and in warring factions. These included:

- The Two Year War (1975–6) triggered by clashes between Palestinian and Christian Phalange riots in inner Beirut.

- The Invasion (*Al-Ijtiyah*), referring to the Israeli invasion in 1982. This episode included a three-month siege and the continuous bombing of Beirut, even though the original Israeli claim (via the Israeli Minister of Defence, Ariel Sharon) was to enter Lebanon only for a few kilometres to create a 'security zone'. The Invasion phase ended with the Israeli withdrawal from Beirut to South Lebanon. At this time there was also the creation of what Israel called a 'security zone' in Lebanon, policed by the South Lebanon Army. This army was paid for, trained and managed by Israel until 2000, when there was a total Israeli withdrawal from Lebanon.

- The War of the Mountain (1983), which involved fighting over Mount Lebanon (or the Shuf Mountain), by Christians and the Druse and the subsequent displacement of the Christian population into what became known as *Al-Sharquiyyeh* (the eastern part). The Christian militias, namely, the Lebanese Forces, were allied to the Israelis during the invasion. When Israel withdrew from the Mountain, it created a power vacuum that was fought over between the Druse and the Christian militias.

- The War of Liberation (*Harb al-Tahrir*) (1988–9). This refers to the war declared in March 1989 by Prime Minister Michel Aoun against Syria, which ended with a cease-fire and the Taif Accords that led to the official end of the Lebanese War in 1991.

- The War of Annihilation (*Harb al-Ilghaa*) (1990), referring to the clash between the Lebanese Army led by Aoun and the Christian militia of Samir Geagea.

Against this complex political canvas of a country engaged in continuous upheaval, many accounts of the war describe the actual fighting that would emerge locally for a few months or a couple of years, as almost always very localized or on one or two fronts at the same time, or internal to each sect (that is, everyone fought everyone, not just Christians fighting against Muslims). Thus, there was intra-Christian fighting, intra-Muslim fighting, intra-Shi'a fighting and intra-Shi'a-Druse fighting, as well as Palestinians and Druse fighting against Christians and Syrians, and Syrians and Druse fighting against Christians, and so on. Ironically, between the 'events' or mini-wars, there were large periods of relative calm, with more or less constant tensions at the internal front lines. The main fighting between the Christian groups involved the different factions of the Maronite Catholics.

The human casualties of the war (approximately 150 000 people were killed and 300 000 were wounded)[4] were enormous for a country of only 3 million inhabitants. Another 700 000 residents were displaced and at least 1 million people emigrated permanently, taking with them valuable minds, energies and capital. By 1990 one-third of Lebanon's population had left the country. The violence also caused great damage to Lebanon's cities, ports and countryside. While the first two years of war (as a cause of the Israeli invasion) witnessed the most extensive damage to the buildings and physical infrastructure (including all strategic functions such as the international airport, sewer systems, electrical grid and telephone lines in Beirut), the cost of destruction in the city alone is estimated to be at least $US10 billion.

As a result, by 1991 Lebanon's economy was burdened by devastated national industries, high unemployment, almost non-existent infrastructure, a radically devalued currency and high inflation. By 1992 the population of Beirut had dropped to around 300 000 as residents fled to other cities in Lebanon or overseas. The old city centre of Beirut, anchored by Martyrs' Square and divided by the Green Line, was the most severely damaged area. Beyhum (1992a: 44) notes that as the centre, one of the most reli-giously mixed areas of the city, was demolished, there was 'a shift in the centre of grav-ity to the outskirts' with residents moving into religiously homogeneous suburbs, or single community ghettos. This shift further fragmented the population along sectarian lines. A related and particularly significant aspect of the destruction of the old city centre was the destruction of the souks, a vibrant and cosmopolitan market section

Figure 4.2
BEIRUT'S DESTROYED DOWNTOWN, 1985

of the former downtown area that had been shared by members of all faiths and sects before the war.

Violent conflict in Beirut ceased in 1990 after a large Syrian military presence was established in the Christian-controlled East Beirut and Mount Lebanon. Political power essentially shifted from Maronite Catholic to Sunni Muslim religious factions under the Taif Agreement.[5] This agreement substantially increased the powers of the Prime Minister, who was required to be a Sunni Muslim under the National Pact, and substantially reduced the authority of the Maronite-held presidency. Lebanon came under Syrian control and, except for the southern security zone claimed by Israel, became a de facto Syrian protectorate with the establishment of a Syrian-sponsored, Muslim-controlled government.

The transition in Lebanon, from a culture of war based on extreme sectarian ruptures to one based on reconciliation, cannot be presumed to be the top priority of the political elites now dominating the Lebanese government. As in all reconstruction situations, the leaders in Lebanese society and government confronted the dual tasks of repairing the physical infrastructure of the country and attempting to pacify the inter-religious conflicts that had been present since the formation of the State of Lebanon in 1943. The unfortunate irony is that, although violent armed conflict ended over a decade ago, many of the complex issues that aggravated relationships among the country's various denominational groups before the onset of civil war still remain unresolved. The reconstruction challenge in Lebanon was to find a reconstruction strategy to bind together the complex issues of a multi-confessional[6] society with seventeen identifiable religious affiliations, and to rebuild the country's financial stability, even though the current cultural and economic crises are continually exacerbated by the difficult political and humanitarian crises in neighbouring Middle East countries, particularly Israel.

The question still exists whether the reconstruction programme has so far only accelerated historic tensions between ethnic groups and transformed the former physical scar of the Green Line into an even larger mental divide across the whole map of Lebanon.

The Green Line

The civil war divided Beirut into east and west sectors, splitting the city along what came to be known as the Green Line, which cut through Martyrs' Square at the centre of the city (Figure 4.3). The Arabic name for this front line is *Khutout at tammas*, which means, more accurately in plural, 'confrontation lines' while, in French, it is referred to as the *ligne de combats* (line of combat). The term, Green Line, as will be discussed in the following chapter on Nicosia, was originally borrowed from the neighbouring partition line in Nicosia drawn to divide Cyprus's capital city in 1963. The first two years of the civil war in Lebanon (1975–77) saw the Green Line become a physical barrier between the main opposing militias in the civil war, including Maronite, Phalangist, Sunni and Shiite Muslim groups. The Green Line terminology also refers to the belt of greenery, which emerged when grass and trees grew in streets and buildings that were destroyed and abandoned in Beirut's buffer zone for the duration of the civil-war years.

As part of the original demarcation line, the Beirut city centre gradually ceased to be a functional city centre as businesses and ministries were looted, buildings were transformed into military positions and the civilian population was forced out. Commercial, banking and business functions in the heart of the city were paralysed; the hotels on its periphery were gutted and the activities in the port came to an end. The east–west divide also deeply affected the commercial and transport networks servicing Beirut: bus lines stopped at the demarcation line; roads were closed and only a few 'gates' were kept open. Goods were searched and taxed; citizens were hindered in their movements or kidnapped on their way to the airport or to the port. Telecommunication and electricity cables were cut between the two sectors and water was distributed to the 'other side' according to the whims of the local militia leaders.

The sectarian division in Beirut rapidly increased as residents in formerly mixed neighbourhoods moved to be on the appropriate side of the Green Line. For example, the

Figure 4.3
THE GREEN LINE CROSSING, BEIRUT 1982

number of Muslims living in 'Christian' East Beirut, who had made up 40 per cent of the 1975 population, dropped to just 5 per cent of the 1989 population. A similar redistribution occurred in West Beirut, where the Christian population dropped from 35 per cent of the total in 1975 to 5 per cent in 1989 (Nasr, 1996: 29). Thus, the enormous psychological and demographic barrier imposed on the metropolitan region of Beirut is still very much in existence today and is also reflected in the recent (2005) bombing assassinations of Christian journalists.

While the Green Line separated the many groups in conflict, many Beirutis have argued that the new 'red line' drawn around Solidere's project boundary is an even sharper line between those who have, and those who do not. Other architectural and political commentators have suggested that Beirut is now, in fact, far more polarized than it was just after the war in 1991. The strong identification of 'East Beirut' and 'West Beirut' as continuing separate geographic entities in the wider urban metropolis indicates how the Green Line concept still pervades the mental map of the city. Michael Davie (1987: 146) comments:

> This military line has existed since the first weeks of the civil war, in 1975, until November 1990. It has conditioned all aspects of life in the city; it has divided populations and given the excuse for massacres, deportations, and destruction; it was the main cause for the disappearance of multi-confessional quarters and their replacement by homogeneous ones.

While it is no longer an active front line of war, the old Damascus Road separating the west (Muslim communities) from the east (Christian communities) still represents a major religious and economic division in the city. The span of contradictions regarding this division in Beirut is profound, as evidenced by interviews undertaken for this study with many actors both included and actively excluded of the reconstruction process. Indeed, the issue is so sensitive that even the ex-Lebanese Prime Minister, Hariri, argued that it is politics, not observable demographic or architectural patterns, that influences people's views on the matter:

> There are people who are saying that the city is divided and those who are saying that it is not. Here I think we are talking about two different things. Those who are saying that it is not divided are telling the truth because when you see the buildings and the roads you can't tell who's living here and there. All cities are divided. This is political and has nothing to do with architecture.[7]

However, the post-war mental geography of Beirut still divides the city even though the official east–west distinction does not exist in current maps of the city. Davie (2002) explains: 'Ideas persist that "West Beirut" is Muslim, fundamentalist, overrun by terrorists, under the control of foreign renegade countries, disorganized, dangerous, and that "East Beirut" is Christian, prosperous, organized, pro-Western, tolerant, and safe.'

City as heart: Solidere as messiah?

The development strategy proposed by Solidere was originally part of a national Lebanese economic recovery project called 'Horizon 2000', created by the Council for Development and Reconstruction. The Horizon plan was part of a national recovery scenario that had the ambitious hope of complete reconstruction and recovery by the year 2007. However, such dates and projections have had to be continually revised following dramatic downturns and swings in the prosperity of Solidere between 1998 and 2002. For example, Solidere's capital value fell by US$20 million (or Leb L35 million) in 2000 but rose again in 2002 owing to the success of commercial and residential rental space in new urban developments such as Saifi Village. Many of the original projects planned by Solidere were postponed in 1999–2000 following the Israeli withdrawal from the south of the country. Arab investment in the region, however, dramatically increased as a result of anti-Arab sentiments in the USA, following the 11 September 2001 attacks on New York. More recently, after a low in the share prices following Hariri's death in 2005, Solidere shares are now (March 2006) at an all-time high of US$24.50.

In attempting to understand the link between politics and architecture in Beirut's reconstruction, it is critical to understand the business alliance between Rafiq Hariri, the post-war Prime Minister of Lebanon, and the Solidere development project. Hariri's rise to political leadership was based on his ability to market an aggressive plan for the economic recovery of Lebanon. Hariri's role as the patron of his country's reconstruction connects to the concept outlined in Chapter 1 of the post-war city as both an impossible challenge, but also a significant political opportunity.

The *Centre Ville* vision for rebuilding central Beirut has been described as Prime Minister Hariri's personal vision for rebuilding Lebanon with a focus on Beirut. This vision closely resembles the development of Dubai, a city constructed on the edge of the desert, right down to the glass-walled towers, privatized marinas, conference centres and skyscraper world trade centre. The motivation behind this vision can be appreciated, at least in part, by Hariri's early life in rural poverty and his rise to wealth:

> Esther: What is the perception of your children towards the reconstruction of Beirut?
> Hariri: They love it now. I was different from them because I was born in Saida to a poor family. So when I used to come to Beirut, I used to see everything different: I used to be

*amazed by everything ... They compare Beirut with Paris and I compare it with
Saida... But when I ask my children now what do they think about Phoenicia [a hotel
building in Beirut] they would say: it's not bad. They don't have the same feeling I have.[8]*

However, Hariri's humble background has not led to an approach to reconstruction
based on concern for people's livelihoods. As Beyhum (1992b: 6) asserts, this is a vision
in which everyone 'submits to the uncontested will of those who control the wealth
and who are the defenders of cultural conservatism. It is a vision of a city broken up
into segregated islands'.

Many 'official' reconstruction accounts also position Hariri as the metaphorical urban
surgeon who pumped blood back in the corroded arteries of his destroyed city, Beirut.
Trawi (2003: 5) comments: 'Once more, history repeated itself. This time, it did at
the hands of Mr Rafiq Hariri. Unfortunately, it repeated itself under virulent criticism
and slandering, reminiscent of the violent hate campaign mounted against Baron
Haussmann during the execution of his development and reconstruction project of
Paris.'

Colonial visions

The post-colonial critiques of Wright (1991) and King (1990) challenge the legitimacy
of the domination of hegemonic political elites in urban planning practices and
city administrations. Wright comments, 'the process of conceiving and implementing
plans for colonial cities reveals European notions about how a good environment –
including their own – should look and function' (Wright 1991: 1). These analyses are
very relevant in understanding the successes and failures of Beirut's current reconstruction plans.

The examination of the Solidere reconstruction plan for Lebanon's capital city must
be placed within a wider context of unexecuted and highly ambitious master plans by
French planners between 1932 and 1991. These colonial visions represent the inap-
propriateness of large-scale foreign planning in a multi-confessional territory such as
Beirut, as well as the subdued and ineffective role that the state has played in
Lebanon's planning history since independence in 1943. As Salaam suggests, in all these
plans, 'the principle of democratic participation is almost non-existent. War, poverty
and neglect of urban problems have pushed the majority of the population into a
submissive lethargy' (Salaam, 1998). The major plans that influenced the current formation and reconstruction of Beirut include:

1   *The Danger plan* (1932) was prepared under the French Mandate by the French
    consulting firm of Frères Danger. This was the first attempt at a comprehensive plan

for the proposed new Lebanese capital. The plan located major circulation routes, zoning densities, street wall regulation and public open space. It is characterized by the dominance of traffic circulation zones and this emphasis on transport is also reflected in a high level of regional understanding of how to connect Beirut to its secondary regional centres, Tripoli and Sidon, and to Damascus.

2   *The Ecochard master plan* (1943) (see Figure 4.4) for the city of Beirut was developed just after Lebanon's independence from France in 1943, when the country experienced a high level of economic prosperity, mainly because of the oil boom in the wider Gulf region. Ecochard was a French planner and his first master plan for Beirut consisted of introducing major traffic arteries, the new city and the *quartiers congestionnaires*. Sarkis describes Ecochard, as 'the French architect and city planner, who would be brought out of the colonial closet. Along with the outlooks of progress and emancipation, he preached through the gridding and zoning, and functional segregation of the land'. Ecochard saw the role of the urban planner as being 'neutral and disinterested in political affairs and urbanism and as a defender of public interest against larger private concerns' (Sarkis, 1993: 112). The Ecochard plan was ultimately limited in its applicability because it concentrated primarily on zoning controls without developing urban regulations governing the future size or location of development.

3   *The General Master Plan* (1952) is significant as it is recognized as the only legal planning strategy still governing metropolitan Beirut. Based upon a plan by the French planner, Egli, it mainly dealt with envisaging new transportation hubs to control future population mobility and decentralization. The plan preceded the Shihab political era of 1958–67, which was a highly prosperous time for Lebanon. The aim was to develop a modern Lebanese society with Beirut as the epicentre of trade and culture in the Arab world. Under Shihab there was a great interest in centralized planning structures to effect change in the wider territorial limits of Beirut's expanding metropolis.

Figure 4.4
ECOCHARD PLAN FOR BEIRUT, 1943

4   *The Plan Directoire Beyrouth et Ses Banlieux* (1964) was also prepared by Ecochard
    and was mainly an effort to deal with the spreading urbanization on Beirut's
    periphery. The plan was never a restrictive one in terms of curbing building devel-
    opment. Indeed, it was limited to projects that never materialized. For example, his
    1943 plan reintroduced a proposed city to the west, along with another new city,
    in order to 'build a healthy city next to an ailing city' (Sarkis and Rowe, 1998: 113).
    The plan determined a zoning strategy but without specifying the perimeter of
    each zone or providing specific urban regulations guiding height and density. The
    Ecochard plan coincided with the creation of the General Directorate of Urban
    Planning and the first town planning legislation applicable to all Lebanon was devel-
    oped as result. It is interesting that at this time, Ecochard also cautioned against
    over-construction and the imminent destruction of the environment – two issues
    that now beset contemporary Beirut.

Post-war master plans for Beirut's reconstruction

Figure 4.5
SOLIDERE MASTER PLAN, 1992

Two master plans (in 1977 and 1992) illustrate the ideological power of the approach
of the 'city as heart' to the reconstruction of the Beirut central district. The first strategy
by the APUR (Atelier Parisien D'Urbanisme) was articulated shortly after the start of
the war, when physical destruction was still limited. As a result, it adopted an approach
based on the preservation of the urban fabric through small-scale and medium-scale
developments by the original owners and with the participation of real estate companies in heavily damaged areas. The 1991 plan (Figure 4.5) was more intrusive and was
to be implemented by a single development corporation. This proposal was faced
with fierce criticism from many opponents. In fact, Solidere had the wisdom to
take into consideration such opposition when it embarked on its reconstruction
programme. Consequently, it made amendments to the 1991 plan and also invited

a number of those who originally opposed that plan (for example, Oussama Kabbani, former Head of Urban Management in Solidere) to participate in the amendment process.

During the first break in the civil war in 1977, the Lebanese government appointed a committee guided by the APUR to draw up a master plan for the largely destroyed central business district of Beirut. In the same year the Ministry of Planning was abolished and the Council for Redevelopment established to oversee the planning, financing and implementation of the rebuilding process. APUR was asked by the Council to propose the first schemes for the redeveloping the city centre, limited to the area that had received most destruction, 1.58 by 1 square kilometres. The philosophy established behind the 1977 strategy was to protect the existing cultural heritage and reject the grand gestures typical of the French mandate, such as wide boulevards. The APUR plan was also predicated on heavy investment in engineering and infrastructure projects and an unlikely scenario of a benevolent public sector to fund the projects. The strategy was approved in 1978, but the resumption of war in 1982 with the Israeli sieges, again delayed any hope for reconstruction. 'Assem', a local architect, has described the impact of the plan in the following way:

> We didn't change the ownership of the fabric of the city. We didn't do anything that traumatized the population or traumatized the fabric of the city and we encouraged people to do the reconstruction themselves, in certain orientations of course. But we encouraged them to come back and we kept the memory of the city still vivid for them to come back. And we improved certain communication areas and we made some renovations to the scale of the city itself.[9]

The aim of the plan was, according to Salaam, to maintain the urban tissue in its original condition wherever possible and to maintain original property tenure, with a secondary aim of encouraging legal owners and occupants of the central business district to return to their previous activities and thus accelerate the return of the *Centre Ville* to its traditional role as a 'unifying ground for Lebanon's multi-confessional communal structure and infrastructure improvements'. (Salaam 1998: 57)

During a truce in 1986 another master plan was drafted by the l'Institut d'aménagement et d'urbanisme de la région Île-de-France (l'AURIF). The plan was developed as a metropolitan vision for accommodating a series of secondary centres to Beirut while still maintaining Beirut as the capital hub in Lebanon. The most problematic aspect of the plan was its solidification of ethnic communities as virtual enclaves by asserting their territorial presence through separate regional centres. Again, the plan, because of the lack of political direction and finance, again like so many others that had preceded it, never materialized.

Figure 4.6
NEW YORK/BEIRUT? ORIGINAL
SOLIDERE MARKETING IMAGES

The 1991 Dar al-Handasah master plan called for reconstruction through a real-estate company (Solidere) with the idea that such a company could make compulsory purchases of land and damaged buildings. This strategy of urban privatization is not particularly new, with the London Docklands and *La Défense* in Paris as other key examples of this mode of project finance.

The reconstruction debate in Beirut thus reflects the tension between two urban design approaches: the 'as it was, where it was' approach and the *tabula rasa* approach of imposing new patterns of order on the destroyed urban centre. It was the latter that was chosen for Beirut.

With half the Solidere stock to be owned by previous owners and half by investors, the company could (theoretically) compensate owners with free shares in the new real-estate company. Prepared by Dar al-Handasah Shair and Partners[10] and French-Lebanese architect, Henri Eddeh, the 1991 master plan focused on the old city centre rather than providing any vision of transforming the city in order to transform the country. A public body, the Council for Development and Reconstruction, initially commissioned the plan, but the private Hariri Foundation, or one of its many subsidiaries, financed it. As has been noted, the new plan provided no scope for integrating the new developments on the periphery of Beirut, which had started to mushroom by the end of war in 1990.

When the 1991 scheme was submitted to the Directorate General of Urbanisme in July 1992, the project came under fierce opposition from architects, planners and journalists. An association of the rightful claimants to downtown property was formed and it also, strongly opposed the project. Apart from issues of property rights and fears of many former residents about not having sufficient capital to buy a home or office in the up-market *Centre Ville* buildings, a major concern was a perceived lack of cultural appropriateness in the proposed urban design and architectural form. The plan was predicated upon the total demolition of the damaged urban fabric in the city centre, creating a new urban scar on the already war-torn city fabric. Many commented wryly

A

Figure 4.7
(A) AND (B) BEIRUT'S NEW
CENTRAL BUSINESS DISTRICT,
2005   B

that the Solidere plan would cause more damage to downtown Beirut than the two previous decades of civil war, all for what Stewart (1991: 67) described as a project 'devoid of memory and a Middle-Eastern version of Canary Wharf' (see Figure 4.7).

While the l'AURIF study was impressive in its methodology and urban analysis, it developed neither concrete projects for consideration nor any private sector mechanism for funding them. In many ways, it continued the same tradition of earlier French colonial planners, such as Ecochard, in assuming that a top-down centralized approach was relevant in planning and that local Lebanese architects and planners had little ability to undertake such studies. For example, 'Eric' comments: 'It is different now from many years ago. Now when the Lebanese government has French people for their expertise it is because [locally] there is no kind of quality, there are no specialists'.[11]

Many architects whom I interviewed in Beirut commented that the Lebanese government never took up the plan as it was perceived to be in competition with the Solidere project. The main purpose of the l'AURIF project was, in fact, to provoke debate and dialogue on the reconstruction problem with the aim of proposing different types of actions, proposing a change of urban rules and moving away from emergency projects. There has, however, been much criticism of the l'AURIF strategy for Beirut, based upon the perception that its authors were a group of outsiders offering inappropriate master plans, and on the belief that the French model of strategic thinking is irrelevant and outdated. As Oussama Kabbani (ex-town planning manager of Solidere) commented on the plan: 'Give me actions. Provide common ground, and give me projects'.[12]

Urban surgery

In a 1995 promotional Solidere video, the background image and the beat of a heart monitor dominate the reconstruction narrative. As I have said, the metaphor of rebuilding the city's heart as akin to a surgical operation on a diseased body dominates the planning and rationale behind much of the rebuilding strategy. In this way it also revives the concept of architects as 'pathologists' described in Chapter 3. On the other hand, Solidere architects supporting this metaphor suggest that:

> Once reconnected it can be the place where the city reconnects; if you want to do business with all Lebanese communities, you need a presence in the city centre and lastly behind the project lies the political will and imperative for it to spearhead Lebanon's national recovery programme and lead the way toward a new international role for Beirut within the region. (Gavin, 1996: 221)

The original Solidere redevelopment plan proposed to restore the symbolic function of the centre by linking the metropolitan region through a series of sunken arteries. Based on the original 1991 master plan, Solidere aimed to optimize the use of the site's waterfront assets and draw on the city's rich archaeological heritage. The project aimed at creating a modern district spreading over 180 hectares of land and reclaiming one-third of this from the sea. There was also a serious goal of promoting social pluralism: 'The neutral grounds of the city centre provide the best possibility for a fresh new beginning. They allow the post-war society to come back without trespassing on another's turf. In short, they have the potential of providing the right infrastructure for the emergence of a pluralist society in Beirut' (Kabbani, 1992: 259).

The 1991 master plan provide an urban design framework for the superstructure and prescribed a mix of land uses within a total development target of 4.69 million square metres of floor space. There were three major aspects to the plan: the redevelopment of the waterfront into a promenade as a continuous corniche; the preservation of 400 low-rise buildings in the central business district to protect the low-rise area, and international competitions to rebuild the souks and nearby housing projects such as the Safi village.

The centrepiece of the Solidere plan is the creation of a new business district on reclaimed land at the northern tip of the original medieval city. Solidere's programme also rehabilitates the Souk (market) area where the civil war began. The reconstruction was planned as a three-phase process over a twenty-two year period. The first phase included the preservation of the city's heritage; the next stage, the modernization of the city centre and, finally, the development and enhancement of the road networks. The business island developed as part of the modernization phase is surrounded by a major ring road effectively separating the planned central business district from the existing city.

The new island, now substantially complete in 2006, contains 4.6 million square metres of mixed-use space with an emphasis on offices, retail, government buildings and leisure and cultural facilities. At present the mix is being influenced by market/investment pressures to place more emphasis on residential building – including second-home residential properties for wealthy Gulf Arabs. According to Solidere planners, pre-sales have been taken on virtually all waterfront sites on the reclaimed land, for delivery in two to four years, 2006–2008.

The critique of Beirut's reconstruction and the role of architects in the rebuilding process can be summarized through five themes that also highlight many of the issues addressed in the following case study of Nicosia and subsequent chapter on Mostar:

- Island mentality

- Legal processes

- Paradise for the rich

- Ruins memorabilia

- Reconstruction as reconciliation?

Island mentality

The creation of Hariri's island is captured in Friedmann's (1987) concept of social polarization. This describes cities as the sites of society's 'winners and losers' and the 'us' and 'them' phenomena intensified by globalization. The Solidere plan was based on the vision of an isolated island or instant city with little consideration of the regional impact of such development or of allocating priority to repairing the immediate war damage outside the former city centre. As 'Assem' comments: 'We are dealing with a divided city, not an island off Saudi Arabia. The reconstruction should have taken a more timid approach – we had other priorities – areas you had to darn, instead of Hariri's projects.'[13]

As I have said in the Solidere scheme, there is a very limited vision of how the reconstruction of the central business district would relate to adjacent regional centres, north and south, and how to accommodate the massive post-war demographic shifts of displaced persons across all Lebanon. The fact that very little public transport was planned, on the assumption that all transport to and from the centre would be by private car, also reinforced the enclave quality of the development. Another reason behind the commercial focus of the Solidere development can be attributed to the confusion of the private with public or informal realms in Arabic culture. In Lebanon, as in other Arab countries, the private and public realms are not distinct categories, a cultural fact which many commentators (Adwan, 2002; Salaam, 1998) see as the main cause of government corruption. Charles Adwan comments:

> The tribal roots of our society confuse what is individual property with what is tribal property. Of course, in the modern age the concept of the tribe was transferred to that of the state. On the other hand, the colonial heritage has brought a sense of alienation towards the public realm due to its association with the colonial or imperial powers. (Adwan, 2002)

This confusion and alienation inevitably leads to a conflict of interest over political and property issues which many have argued is characteristic of Solidere. In a situation where a prime minister could introduce a law delegating the appropriation of public and private property to a company that he partially owned, a conflict of interest is unavoidable. Again, by isolating the city centre from its wider metropolis, the segregation patterns imposed by the civil war have been deepened and extended.

The vast social discrepancies and lack of equitable development in the prewar era both fuelled and catalysed the original outbreak of the war. The creation of Solidere emphasized these social discrepancies by sealing off an island of wealth on the debris of what used to be a middle-class area that had been weakened by the war and annihilated by post-war policies. Instead of returning the displaced to their homes, Solidere contributed to the displacement of the original inhabitants of the city centre, even though many of them had been relocated at the start of the war owing to intense fighting in the area. This was accomplished without public participation or accountability. Many of the original tenants were forced to give up their property rights in exchange for shares or their equivalent, based on a questionable assessment and evaluation process. If they had decided to keep their property, the conditions set by Solidere would have cost them far more than the property was worth. On the other hand, their shares would have been subject to the market fluctuations linked to the association of Solidere with Hariri's position in power. Ownership of these shares would allow limited participation in the decision- making process, given that the majority of shares had been sold before the process took place. All this clearly left the decision-making powers with rich investors who are not necessarily Beirutis.

Seeing the post-war field as an opportunity to create an instant oasis for the privileged in a site which has no relationship to the regional context is thus a strong metaphor for the central business district project in Beirut. Davie comments in relation to Beirut's reconstruction: 'A city cannot be reduced to its material dimension, nor can it be simply related to its economic functions. It is both *significant* and *signifié*, a coded object, which its societies continuously appropriate, territorialize, and re-territorialize according to numerous collective or individual stakes' (Davie, 2002).

Since undertaking the research for this book there has been a growth of business, tourism and land prices, during 2004–2006, on the Solidere boundary in the areas of Ain Mraysse and Gemayze. The central business district development, however, has not allowed for economically mixed neighbourhoods that include upper-, middle- and lower-income inhabitants. Solidere hopes that around 40 per cent of the built-up area in the city centre will become residential. The other 60 per cent consists primarily of offices, commercial facilities, cultural facilities and hotels. Most people living in the central district currently belong to upper-income groups. Limiting mass access to the city centre in this way prevents the revival of what used to be one of the few areas of coexistence in Lebanon. And, of course, by coexistence is meant that of communities and social groups, not the wealthy merchant groups who make up only a small minority of the Lebanese population.

Following this argument, the sequence of master plans provided since 1975 has provided increasingly less possibility for private individuals to reappropriate a variety of urban functions in the former *Centre Ville* area. For example, in the 1977 project, former landowners were financially responsible for the rehabilitation of up to 75 per cent of the land. In the 1986 project, this role was gradually shifted to the state, while by 1991 financing was located in the hands of the private conglomerate, Solidere. This process has largely excluded the middle-class residents from reinvesting in their properties.

Using the rebuilding process as a tool for reconciliation beyond the concept of a privileged oasis could have been possible only by dispersing the reconstruction efforts beyond the boundaries of the *Centre Ville* and by public participation in a sequence of smaller residential, infrastructural and cultural development projects, exemplified in the Nicosia reconstruction process detailed in the next chapter. Or, as Ayssar Arrida suggests: 'Of course my own solution would have gone for a much more 'fractal' boundary, taking Solidere beyond the ring, and bringing the 'messy bits' inside the ring, thus obliging a higher degree of osmosis and of mutual catalysis of development.'[14]

The idea that Oussama Kabbani presents, that 'these complex problems could not have been resolved by individual efforts, nor through piecemeal reconstruction efforts' (Kabbani, 1998: 247), is therefore questionable and favours only those wealthy enough to have benefited from the development company he worked with for nearly a decade. The challenge is rather to ask how, as architects, we should mark the difference between what was, what happened and what should be. As architecture student Bilal,[15] comments:

> Of all the ruins of troubles and conflicts inflicted by insiders and outsiders in Beirut, one tangible reality stands out; tiny changes in our everyday environments can radically alter the quality of our lives, and individuals can at least be re-socialized to perceive differences not as symptoms of distrust, fear and exclusion but as manifestations of cultural diversity and enrichment.

The rush to establish Solidere and its associated privatized planning process in order to reinvent a prosperous international image for the destroyed city of Beirut, has then only further divided an already highly fractured post-war nation-building process.

Legal processes

Most criticisms of the Solidere project focus not so much on an aesthetic critique of the rebuilding but, rather, on the dubious legal processes that gave the Beirut municipal administration authority to create a real-estate company in war-damaged areas. In this, the role of the city's political administration was reduced to the formation of a development company and the marking of physical boundaries for the new reconstructed Solidere island. Solidere was originally configured as a conglomeration of property-right holders, private Lebanese (many in the diaspora) and Arab investors.

The issue of managing property rights in reconstructing the downtown area has also raised serious questions concerning the lack of democratic planning processes that were undertaken by rebuilding agencies in the fast-track development of Beirut. It is estimated that in the central business district alone there were an estimated 100 000 claimants on 1630 parcels of land (Beyhum, 1992a). Many claims predate the civil war and claimants range from individual householders to large Western companies that once had offices there. Lebanese property laws further complicated the process where individuals holding leases to a property and actual owners of the property both have property rights. In addition, many former building owners have died since the beginning of the civil wars and their property has been left to families residing both inside and outside Lebanon.

In order to deal with this complex web of property rights, the Lebanese Parliament introduced 'Law 117' in 1991, granting Solidere the legal power to expropriate the property of existing owners. In return, whether they liked it or not, property owners received shares in Solidere. According to one Solidere resident whom I interviewed in 2001, landholders received 65 per cent of the total number of Solidere shares, with an estimated value of US$1.2 billion. Solidere's remaining shares, valued at US$650 million, were then sold to the Lebanese public to raise cash for infrastructure. In 1999 Hariri held 19 per cent of the company's shares (with his wife and children holding even more). Solidere was originally planned as a conglomeration of property right holders and private Lebanese investors. Again, the consequent reduction of the state to a private investor rather than overseeing authority is perhaps the most contentious and problematic aspect of the redevelopment strategy. In addition to planning critics and journalists, residents adjacent to the Solidere neighbourhood resent the redevelopment process, as indicated by 'Raymond', a resident of East Beirut:

> Esther: What do you feel about Solidere?
> Raymond: It is just a successful company, but it should not have been privatized. The government should have required the reconstruction of some of those buildings by their owners according to a pre-set plan and not forced them to sell them. Just 10 minutes ago, a friend of mine told me that he was forced to sell three buildings that he had before the war in the city centre for $15 000 only. They destroyed his life. What can he do with this money? Buy a car? Fifteen thousand is still not enough [to buy a car]. They destroyed many people.[16]

As a consequence, many landowners protested against the Solidere expropriation scheme and, according to Fisk (1990), it was not only the Christian and Muslim elite landowners who opposed government expropriation of property rights. The Iranian-backed fundamentalist Shi'a Muslim group, Hezbollah, has also spoken out against Solidere, stating that Islamic law protects people from surrendering their property against their will. The issue of lack of consultation with either residents or the general public was also one of the major issues underlying a popular outcry against the reconstruction project in its early days. Unlike previous strategies for the city's redevelopment (like the 1977 APUR plan, which emerged during a break in the fighting), the current plan proceeded largely without any participation, especially from the middle class. According to Beyhum (1992a: 101) 'Residents have found their role in a reconstructed Beirut to be shrinking. This lack of involvement is especially discouraging because a reconstruction plan for Beirut, in which religious groups work together, could help form the basis for a stronger, more unified, post-war Lebanon.'

Another objection to the proposed law was the perceived lack of justice for many original owners who, while they had been given the choice of reoccupying their properties, could not afford to do so. They could not abide by the predetermined completion timetable and strict conservation standards demanded by Solidere. According to 'Abdul',[17] a former resident of the central business district area, little assistance was offered to allow former residents to pay for or borrow money for such reconstruction. This is a particular concern that, in making the Centre Ville area an island for the rich, the majority of those working in the city centre will be excluded. Most city-centre workers are not corporate heads, but middle- and low-income employees involved in service jobs.

Finally, while legally speaking, Solidere is a private company; the nature of its work has a high level of public interest. Indeed, it has fallen over the roles that many public agencies should have been doing. Solidere, however, is not subject to any controlling agency or mechanism that ensures the preservation of public interest such as in the case of public institutions. In other words, Solidere is a privatized project, where the privatization has been done with little consideration for standards of transparency, accountability and the protection of citizens' rights, for inviting their participation or for them to prevent conflicts of interest. In effect, Solidere, which was supposed to be a way around the inefficient red tape and paralysis of the public bureaucracy, ended up functioning just like a public bureaucracy for former land owners wishing, but financially unable, to rebuild on their own soil. In this way, it also reflects Barakat's (1998: 13) view that 'physical reconstruction programmes often reinforce existing social divisions'.

Paradise for the rich?

> Well, we come back to what we started before: was the reconstruction of the downtown centre the top priority for them? After seventeen years of war in an area which the population had vacated, was it the top priority? And even if it were, what we should have done was another question to ask?[18]

The 1990 decision to treat the central business district as a privatized real-estate project created what Assem Salaam terms a 'paradise for the rich that you needed to enter with a credit card through the Solidere stage design'.[19] In fact, *Centre Ville* became

Figure 4.8
VERSACE COMES TO BEIRUT

a spectacular project for tourists wanting to see for themselves the miracle of post-war Beirut.

Adding to concerns that the Hariri-led government was creating 'an island for the rich', a series of government-initiated infrastructure and entertainment projects were developed in parallel with the expensive' commercial, retail and residential developments in the central business district. These included the Cité Sportif Stadium, a new $US1 billion international airport and a new highway from the airport to the central business district. While the Cité Sportif Stadium is rarely used, the airport and highway projects are adjacent to the Ouzai area, which is largely inhabited by poor Christian and Muslim residents living in shantytowns next to the airport but who have no occasion to use it.

Although the redevelopment of Beirut's southern suburbs, specifically the Elyssar project, began in the 1990s and included the construction of 7250 housing units, schools and hospitals, much of the poor population remains unserviced. In terms of integrating the various confessional and social groups in Lebanese society, the central business district renewal project claims to be offering a new gathering centre for the various populations in Lebanese society. However, the Solidere development has not focused on integrating these populations through giving priority to re-establishing public space zones.

Interviews in Beirut with residents close to the new central business district and former Green Line support this view of the city as an increasingly exclusive entity, not one to be shared by everyone:

> Esther: Do you think it would become like it used to be before the war?
> Salma: Only the physical construction would be repaired but the rest will remain poor and marginalized. You lived the war and you know what it's like.
> Esther: Does it represent you?
> Salma: No it doesn't: anything that represents everybody represents me and anything that represents a specific branch of the population doesn't represent me. What would the new city centre mean to me when I can't go there?[20]

Prime Minister Hariri did not dispute the view of the Solidere island as a paradise for the rich. 'Two-thirds of this land is residential; about three million square metres are residential with 30 000 apartments, so if we have rich people to fill 30 000 apartments, it means that we're in a good position.'[21]

This contrasts with the situation in Beirut's southern suburbs where the Islamic group Hezbollah has secured a following among the poor by providing a level of social infrastructure, including low-cost housing and schools. Yet, when interviewed again in 2004, Solidere planners still optimistically saw the central business district project as a major success and spoke of the fashionable shopping and restaurants and proposals for a Formula One racing circuit in the former downtown area. Indeed, after 9/11 a whole new clientele of local Lebanese and Arab tourists have returned to the region. In reconstructing the former bourgeois playground of *Centre Ville*, a revived new economy has been generated, which may in time compete again with Tel Aviv and Larnica as major centres of tourist and commercial activity. A Planning official also suggests that Beirut 'needed a vision, a story' and that 'the name of the game is to attract investment'.[22] This type of uncritical acceptance of their own story means that senior planning officials continue to ignore many of the problems remaining in Beirut. Typical of them is 'Joseph' from the Directorate of Urbanism who says, 'The city is not divided. There are no problems for anyone to come back. The situation is quite normal'.[23]

It can therefore be argued that in current reconstruction strategies in Beirut, the values of Putnam's (1991; 1995) concept of social capital have been displaced by those of material success. As I have said, a disastrous aspect of Beirut's reconstruction is the government's failure to tackle the pressing needs of the poor half of population, such as the concentration of squatters in the southern suburbs of Beirut. Small amounts of capital have been directed towards areas like Saida (the home town of the late Prime Minister Hariri), and famous tourist sites like Tyre, but there has been limited reconstruction of infrastructure or improvement of the living standards of non-Beiruti residents, except in a few wealthy inner-city areas such as Achrafieh, since before the civil war began.

Ruin memorabilia

The war has not only destroyed common spaces and reinforced proclivities for the formation of exclusive and seclusive enclaves. It has also generated a mood of lethargy and indifference which borders, at times, on collective amnesia. (Khalaf, 1993: 19)

Can buildings, landscape projects and re-created souks help war-destroyed urban centres recover their spirit? Establishing what people choose to remember and what people choose to forget has a direct relationship with how we, as architects, can begin to restructure the urban fractures and landscapes we are asked to reconfigure and re-imagine in the post-war scenario. In Beirut the issues of conservation and reconstruction are tied to the policy of 'destructive construction' with a political will to modernize and an economic will to join the world economy.

Figure 4.9
ROMAN RUINS NEXT TO SOLIDERE DEVELOPMENT SITE

The cliché of the 'memory of the city' has been used and abused during the past decade both by advocates and opponents of the reconstruction of the business central district. This popular marketing invocation of 'memory' is questionable when nearly 85 per cent of the buildings in downtown Beirut were razed before development by Solidere had even begun. Each group has tailored the notion of 'collective memory' to fit with its own needs and arguments. One will naturally be presented with a variety of reactions to the reconstruction of the city centre, and no generalizations can be made about the 'memory of the city' and the suitability of its reconstruction, despite what is often asserted by planners, designers and politicians.

Much of the justification of the Solidere strategy focuses on the importance of re-creating 'segments of memory' from Beirut's long and rich list of archaeological sites. This is reflected in the images of Beirut that dominate its marketing brochures. Beirut is portrayed as a trading crossroads and cultural watershed between Europe and the East. However, at least two concerns may be noted about the reality behind such rhetoric. The first relates to the relatively minor priority accorded during the reconstruction to Beirut's archaeological significance. Indeed, although only 10 per cent of the central business district has been excavated by archeologists, Solidere is now selling parcels of land in the central business district for development, which will reduces the chance for any significant further archaeological exploration.

According to many local architects, Solidere wanted the excavations to be as short as possible and restricted the archaeological zone to specific areas so as not to hinder the rebuilding process. Whatever was found, of whatever epoch, could eventually be integrated in the project, thus exploiting its cultural or tourist value and thereby increasing the land value of the plots. While it was apparently neutral, this position was, in fact, deeply affected by political and personal pressure put on Solidere and on the excavation operations. This pressure, from particular owners of certain plots, aimed to safeguard their interests so that delays or legal action over the archaeological finds would not affect them.

Reconstruction as reconciliation?

American philosopher Robert Putnam discusses the desirable link between social capital, democracy and the development of a civil society (Putnam, 1995). If Putnam's formula for establishing a civil society is one kind of benchmark for successful post-war reconstruction, Beirut's rebuilding processes and products have failed through disempowering marginal groups from participating in the reconstitution of their country and society. In Beirut, reconstruction master plans developed since 1991 have tended to ignore the necessity for urban integration and to deepen the divisions, disunity and segregation existing between different regions and social classes. As we have seen, the low priority placed upon the connection of the developed area to other parts of Beirut's centre (for example, Hamra) though public space linkages, and the dominance of office and retail buildings to which access is available, are proof of this exclusion. Adding to this lack of reconciliation is the question of Palestinian immigration, one of the initial causes of the original civil war. In 2003, approximately 400 000 Palestinians still remained in Lebanon, with 200 000 still in refugee camps bordering the city, comprising nearly 10 per cent of the total population of the country.[24]

The central business district plan therefore became a development propaganda piece about an exclusionary island framed by a development 'pole' concept. For example, three parallel north–south roads including a large avenue 10 metres wider than the Champs-Elysees in Paris, constituted the first 'pole'. It could be argued that the original projected US$18 million cost of the central business district project could have been spent more sensibly on developing a metropolitan vision to strengthen the polycentric structure surrounding Beirut by renewing weak infrastructure connections and links.

In summary, Beirut's reconstruction is not a total failure. It gave many Lebanese some semblance of hope that the war was finally over and that the prosperous days they had enjoyed in the 1960s would come again. Beirut architect 'Robert' commented regarding the central business district renewal: 'People are more powerful than corporations, and … eventually they will take over the city and its centre.' Much of the condemnation of the project stems from a critique of the central planning metaphor of the heart, from which the life-blood of economic prosperity would spread, once the project had successfully re-created downtown Beirut as the Paris of the East, once again the social, tourism and entertainment capital (and banking centre) of the eastern Mediterranean. However, the metaphor of the heart was defective as the political and economic goals that underpinned it failed to address the social, cultural and religious divisions that were the root causes of the original civil war.

Most architects in Lebanon thus largely failed to campaign for the opportunities that post-conflict reconstruction provides for creating new patterns of equitable and sustainable urban development, design and infrastructure that could have somehow bridged together the divided communities of Beirut. Using the 'city as spine' concept for Beirut's reconstruction would have been a more appropriate planning metaphor than 'city as heart', as it could have guided the development of urban patterns that linked communities and could have given a backbone to the peace process. The 'spine' method would have entailed implementing a series of smaller-scale infrastructural, residential and commercial projects across the entire Beirut region, rather than just its centre.

This lack of innovation in post-war architectural practice in the country is particularly disappointing, as architects in the Middle-East region are generally accorded high status, as part of a professional 'holy trinity' of doctors, lawyers and engineers–architects. However, a culture of elitism combined with a tradition of colonialism, and deferring to foreign experts who come in and tell locals 'what to do', still permeates the design profession in Beirut. Thus, many architects in the country are inclined to position themselves as 'design engineers' serving the economic and political elite without alienating potential clients through strategic thinking about the location and social rationale of certain forms of building development over others. As Tabet (1998: 99)noted: 'Indeed what is striking about the architects' attitudes during these glorious years is their lack of concern for political issues, their ignorance of the real forces that were struggling to strengthen their control over territories.'

Despite provocative work by many young Beirut architects, such as Bernard Khoury, and the occasional conferences organized by the Lebanese Order of Engineers and Architects, there has been a critical lack of debate on Beirut's reconstruction since the mid-1990s. While there was much protest in the early days of Solidere's formation by citizens groups, Beiruti journalist 'Elias'[25] attributes the lack of discourse a decade on from the cessation of the war, not so much to a lack of interest in the built environment but, rather, to sheer exhaustion and malaise among architects and journalists. He says, 'all the big and interesting names in Lebanese architecture were part of the campaign against Solidere', and argues that, 'After that, Solidere was done. You cannot destroy it. It was political power and money. Everybody was tired after the war'.

In Lebanon today there are still few architectural awards, design competitions or architectural magazines, and little critical commentary. The design and construction industries are still dominated by engineers, and any adherence to Lefebvre's rule of 'right to the city' is limited to designing large city buildings and empty residential villas. The lack of debate among the large number of practising architects and architecture schools in Lebanon (4000–5000 architects and seven architecture schools in a population of more than 3 million in the country) is particularly surprising.

Similarly, the urban planning profession in Lebanon has proposed few alternative visions for the country at a local or regional scale. The model of the French *beaux-arts* 'urban surgery' approach is still popular in existing planning degrees and there is little focus on developing new planning methods for the specific conditions of Middle East cities. Instead, a clear focus on the physical dimension of planning with few economic or social parameters still guides the real-estate market in Beirut, reinforcing the role of architects and planners as colonialists once again. In summary, architects and planners in Lebanon seem politically unengaged, with little commitment to using their profession as an agent for social or cultural change. Whereas in Berlin after the Cold War there was fierce debate about issues of architecture as a tool for social reconciliation via the 'Stadtforum' (city debates) process, there is virtually no debate in Lebanon on issues of urban heritage or social justice, and their relationship to the peace process and the design profession.

Thus, within the broader framework of the role of design professionals after conflict, the role of architects in Lebanon can be viewed as aligned more closely with the pathologist, hero, colonialist and historicist models than those of social reformers, educators and leaders of popular opinion. As pathologists, Beiruti architects and their patrons (Hariri) viewed the city as a body whose heart needed reconstructive surgery. As heroes, they vied for contracts to build remembrance structures as part of one-off architectural or landscaping projects, such as the 'Gardens of Forgiveness', or to rebuild former segments of downtown Beirut, such as the 1994 competition to redevelop the souks, won by Spanish architect Rafael Moneo, and the more recent 2004 Solidere competition to redevelop Martyrs' Square.

As historicists, architects acted as nostalgic conservers of culture heritage through Solidere projects such as building Saifi Village as a postmodern pastiche. In so doing, Lebanese architects largely neglected opportunities to adopt roles such as educators (by educating the public and refocusing architectural, design and planning education), social reformers (by seeking to facilitate social integration through appropriate urban design) and public intellectuals (through engaging actively in political mediation and facilitating community participation in planning and reconstruction).

Lessons learnt

Three major themes can be identified related to the opportunities and constraints of the post-war reconstruction process in Beirut:

1   *Lack of public consultation.* The substantive lack of public consultation processes employed in reconstruction projects for Beirut indicates the dominance of the private sector in all development issues, creating a pervasive politics of exclusion.

Because the rebuilding of Beirut has been left entirely in the hands of Solidere, any broader planning strategies for the whole region of Lebanon, as one would assume would play a central role of the post-conflict environment, have been largely absent. Increased democracy in the planning and design processes, as illustrated earlier in Berlin's models of the Stadtforum is thus clearly necessary to the healthy functioning of all cities, divided or not.

2 *Apolitical architecture.* Lebanese architects have become increasingly reluctant to engage in the larger political and lobbying processes in providing planning and design alternatives to either Beirut or smaller regional centres. The role of the architect in Lebanon is directly targeted towards pleasing the client rather than questioning polit-ical processes impinging on the built environment. One local architect suggested that 'if the destruction of the central district of Beirut during fifteen years of civil war has been an agonizing experience for Lebanese citizens, the plan for its reconstruction has exposed them to an intolerable vision of their capital's future'.[26] Architects involved in Beirut's reconstruction could then be seen as accomplices in the largest privatized reconstruction project in the world, creating a kind of Versacesque Disneyland. Setting up a listed company – Solidere – to manage the post-war recon-struction of a central business district is unprecedented in spirit and scale. Lebanon's competitive, free-market approach to the acquisition of professional guidance brought to the table the best talent that money could buy, in true post-colonial style. Finally, Beirut, as discussed above, presents many warning beacons for rebuilding future war-damaged cities, including the dangers of a total reliance upon the private sector in funding and administering the rebuilding programme and in focusing the post-war redevelopment exclusively in the central city area. The exclusive island that Solidere created largely benefits only those Lebanese and foreign tourists wealthy enough to enjoy it.

3 *Process over product.* Further analysis of the post-war terrain in Lebanon suggests that the orthodox master plan approach is questionable when there is not a defin-able government reconstruction agency in the country. Smaller incremental pilot projects, (as we will see in the next chapter on Nicosia's reconstruction) may have been more appropriate models in stimulating investment and reconstruction inside and outside Beirut. As related to the more general investigation of cities polarized by ethnic conflict, what emerges out of most observations on Beirut's reconstruc-tion is that it has been the process of rebuilding (for example, the controversial process of land expropriation employed by Solidere in the former downtown) that is objectionable, rather than the material end product of the *Centre Ville* project.

In conclusion, it is hard to argue against the Solidere development on the grounds of financial and commercial prosperity (for investors and stakeholders in the company and as a destination for international tourists) and Hariri's enormous vision for rebuild-ing his country. As one Beiruti colleague commented: 'I truly believe that there has not been a "better" way (at that time) to get what was necessary to be done within the time frame without his guidance (even if not a "well-educated" one)'. It is very impor-tant, however, to recognize the social cost of this prosperity. The ends do not always justify the means. Adam Smith spoke of an 'invisible hand of enlightened self-interest' (Smith, 1998). Beirut architects and policy-makers have, therefore, to be careful not to cause this hand to materialize and sweep away all that stands in its way. The question, therefore, is not so much whether Beirut will ever regain its former position as the broker between the West and the Middle East but, rather, how can it rebuild its own still profoundly divided social fabric?

The next case study, on Nicosia, provides a more positive example of the capacity of architects to work in an interdisciplinary and consensual mode in resolving the social dilemmas of the post-war city phenomenon.

Notes

1   There are many academics who deal with the specific historical and political causes behind this war in more detail than I do here (Beyhum, 1992a; Fawaz, 1983; Hourani, 1995; Khalaf and Khoury, 1993; Salaam, 1994; Tueni, 1992).

2   Solidere was originally set up as a Lebanese joint-stock company, May 1994.

3   The concept of the 'war of others' relates directly to *La guerre des autres* by Ghassan Tueni, head of *An Nahar* newspaper, ex-Lebanese ambassador to the United Nations and currently a Minister of Parliament owing to his son's assassina-tion in 2005. In this book he investigates the role of non-Lebanese factions, the Cold War and the mutual denial of responsibility. See Tueni (1992).

4   Source: Khalaf (1993).

5   In September 1989, sixty-two of the seventy survivors of the ninety-nine member National Assembly met at the town of Taif in Saudi Arabia to work out a modified version of the Lebanese Constitution. For details of the Taif Agreement see <http://www.mideastinfo.com/documents/taif.htm>.

6   In the literature on Lebanon, 'confessional groups' is the standard usage. The term 'religions' is not acceptable, because the word does not indicate that even within a religion (Christianity or Islam, for example,) a great number of groups exist.

7   Interview with Hariri, June 2000.

8   Interview with Hariri, June 2000.

9   Interview with Assem, June 2000, Beirut.

10 Dar Al-Handasah Shair & Partners is a leading Middle-East planning and development bureau.

11 Interview with Eric, May 2001.

12 Interview with Oussama Kabbani, June 2000.

13 Interview with Assem, June 2000, Beirut.

14 E-mail correspondence with Ayssar Arrida, July 2002.

15 Student Bilal (master of urban design student) 'Position paper', American University of Beirut: Divided City Seminar, March 2000.

16 Interview with Raymond, East Beirut resident, June 2000.

17 Interview with architect, Abdul, Beirut, 2000.

18 Interview with Assem, June 2000, Beirut.

19 Interview with Assem, June 2000, Beirut.

20 Interview with Salma, East Beirut resident, 2000.

21 Interview with Hariri, June 2000.

22 Angus Gavin comments at 'City debate', American University of Beirut, April 2002.

23 Interview with Joseph, Directorate of Urbanism, Beirut, June 2000.

24 See <www.un.org/unrwa/refugees/lebanon.html>.

25 Interview with journalist, Elias, June 2000.

26 Interview with Robert, architect, June 2000.

5

Nicosia – reconstruction as resolution

Figure 5.1
AUTHOR PEERING THROUGH DIVIDING WALL,
NICOSIA 2000

I hope that one day I will see my city functioning like a normal city. If someone tells me that a solution has been reached and that Nicosia has been reunited, in as little as 48 hours, I can remove the obstacles and barriers.

(Lellos Demetrides)[1]

This chapter focuses on the case study of Nicosia through the theme of 'design as resolution', that is, a resolution between the Greek and Turkish Cypriot groups still separated by the island's Buffer Zone. In this second case study I explore the role of architects and planners in envisioning an undivided Nicosia through the planning mechanisms of the Nicosia master plan (NMP). The Buffer Zone is 180 kilometres long and covers around 3 per cent of the island's surface area. It varies in width from less than four metres within the city of Nicosia to nearly 7 kilometres near the village of Athienou. There are five inhabited villages, and around 8000 people who live and work in the Buffer Zone. The Zone has divided northern and southern Cyprus since civil conflict began on the island in the 1960s. The barrier of the Buffer Zone became known as the 'Green Line' where it cut through the actual city of Nicosia.

Unlike Mostar and Beirut, the other two polarized cities examined in this book, Nicosia has suffered neither major physical destruction nor major human casualties during nearly forty years of division.[2] Commenting on the paradoxical nature of this situation, Miran Rechter[3] comments that 'where in Bosnia the Dayton Peace Agreement feels like war, in Nicosia there is no formal peace agreement but it feels like peace', even though there is one soldier for every fifteen inhabitants on the island of Cyprus.

Nicosia still holds the unenviable title of the 'world's last divided city'.[4] It is also the only one of the reconstruction case studies examined with a multidisciplinary and bi-communal approach and a community-based master plan for the current and, perhaps, continuing future state of physical partition. Despite this master plan, however, the centre of Nicosia still remains almost completely partitioned and its Buffer Zone was first surveyed only in 2002, after twenty-eight years of neglect. As one journalist comments: 'Forgotten by foreign professionals, frozen in place by third-party interventions, monitored by two armies and the United Nations, scarred by blighting and dereliction on both sides of the interface, the capital of Cyprus remains crippled both physically and functionally' (Smith and MacAsKill, 2002: 8–10).

Background to partition

It is difficult to write a short summary of the history of the Cyprus conflict. In fact, there are many histories, and even using the label 'conflict' will often meet with sharp reactions. Cultural anthropologist Papadakis (2002: 34) comments: 'The idea that different societies articulate different histories shows, in the context of historical preservation, that history may be severely contested within a single society.'

Both in the academic literature and amongst politicians, the situation on the island is mostly referred to as the 'Cyprus problem' (Hocknell, 2001; Papadakis, 2002). The assumption of a 'paradise history' – that Greek and Turkish Cypriots used to live together peacefully, that they were 'different but friends' – is widespread, not only among modern-day proponents of Cypriot membership of the European Union (EU), but also among many interviewees who largely blame the conflict on external

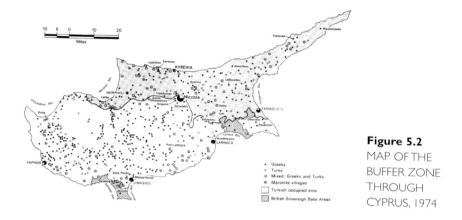

Figure 5.2
MAP OF THE
BUFFER ZONE
THROUGH
CYPRUS, 1974

or international powers. The terminology used to describe the Cyprus conflict is also problematic (for example, a 'martyr' to one group is a 'murderous rebel' to another). As Madeleine Garlick[5] observes: 'I just know what a minefield this terminological landscape is for someone who doesn't deal with it all day every day. My boss says that Cyprus is a "graveyard for good words"… and he is probably right.'

A brief history of the partition can be traced back as far as 1571 when the Ottoman Turks ruled Cyprus for over three centuries, before ceding it to Britain in 1878. Independence from British rule was achieved in August 1960. Many historians have commented that Cyprus's new constitution was an unacceptable compromise between the British and the competing Greek and Turkish communities, among whom considerable distrust remained.

In July 1974, the distrust intensified when President Makarios was deposed by a military coup (allegedly backed by the military regime then in power in Greece). Within days, Turkish troops arrived on the northern coast of Cyprus, having been 'invited' by the Turkish Cypriot leader, Rauf Denktash, to intervene in order to protect the Turkish community on the island. The demarcation line separating the Greek and Turkish quarters of Nicosia ('The Mason-Dixon Line' as it was nicknamed) thus left many Greeks and Turks on the wrong side, with each community at the mercy of the local majority (Cranshaw, 1978: 293). Conflict lasted for eight weeks, during which time British troops had to maintain the separation between the antagonists along a Green Line in mid-Nicosia. As Papadakis (2002) explains, Greek Cypriots were seeking union with Greece (*enosis*) while Turkish Cypriots had been voicing their own demands for the division of the island (*taksim*).

After the Turkish army had taken control of the northern third of the island, a ceasefire was arranged under United Nations (UN) auspices. In November 1983, the Turkish part of the island proclaimed itself independent. The island has remained partitioned ever since and UN peacekeeping forces still maintain a truce between the two sides.

Drawing the Green Line

The Green Line legitimized the separation of the two main communities, providing a 'chinagraph frontier', which was soon to outlive its original purpose of ensuring a workable but temporary, ceasefire.

> The partition that still divides the historic centre of Nicosia has a long lineage. In medieval maps of the city a line that represented a river crosses the then walled Nicosia. However, it was British Major-General Peter Young who established the Nicosia Green Line in 1963 when trying to quell street fighting between Turkish and Greek militias in the capital city. He is said to have taken a green pencil and bisected a map of Nicosia from one side of the old fortifications to the other. Although nearly thirty years have passed since the original conflict began, northern and southern barricades still define the 'dead zone', 20–50 metres of abandoned houses and debris that have remained virtually untouched since 1974. Nicosia's Buffer Zone also runs along the former commercial strip of Hermes Street. This street had been a market or 'souk' from approximately 10 BCE to 1912. Ironically, according to Papadakis, 'Hermes' was the classical Greek god of trade who often transgressed the boundaries of foreign territory. (Hocknell, 2001: 141)

While the dividing line is clearly demarcated on current tourist maps of both Greek and Turkish Nicosia, the barricades that created almost a 'Berlin Wall' across the city are beginning to break down in places. As 'George', a taxi driver in Nicosia comments:

> You see an opening here and an opening there, across a distance of 400 metres or more … there is no barbed wire over here or there. That is why accidents happen all the time. There is no place where you can see a barbed wire going from one side to the other. You can just go for miles and you see nothing.[6]

Since 1974, there have been two spatially distinct and mono-ethnic zones across Cyprus. The divided Greek and Turkish Cypriot entities (as in Mostar) have developed two separate administrations, economies, airports, transportation networks and social organizations. Before the partition, northern Cyprus had occupied territory containing most of the fertile agricultural land on the island and containing the larger portion of tourist attractions and manufacturing facilities. The late 1970s and early 1980s were years of adjustment in which partition was like an open wound crying out to be healed. The two sides had to adjust and plan how to deal with their damaged quasi territories.

In addition to the development of this dual landscape, the two sectors had to solve many problems of infrastructure. For example, many of the areas on the Greek side adjacent to the Green Line have been affected by the partition because of the interruption of irrigation, communications and markets.

The Nicosia master plan

There should be close cooperation between the two sides for the purpose of examining and finally reaching conclusions for a master plan of Nicosia. (UNDP, 1984: 1)

Figure 5.3
THE NICOSIA MASTER PLAN, 1984

The Nicosia master plan forms the major strategic document guiding the investigation of design projects for the city and is thus the basis for evaluating the concept of 'design as reconciliation' in the capital city of Cyprus. The development of the master plan began in 1979 when the Greek Cypriot and Turkish Cypriot leaders of Nicosia, Lellos Demetriades and Mustafa Akinci, agreed on a planning vision for the city under the auspices of the United Nations Development Programme (UNDP). Demetriades then commented that 'Nicosia is not a functional body, it is sick, this is not normal'.[7]

During the process of drawing up the NMP, a close working relationship was established between Demetriades and Akinci. In determining suitable prototypes for their own spatial urban and political dilemma, the two mayors visited Berlin together three times in order to meet urban planners and city officials there. Such a visit by the two leaders suggests the relevance of the comparative case study method by both researchers and key divided city politicians. Demetriades commented about this trip: 'Divided Berlin was for me the most important experience which made me even more keen to pursue the idea of a joint master plan.'[8] Demetriades still rests confident that within forty-eight hours of a formal agreement of peace, the island can be reunited and the Green Line torn down as quickly as the dismantling of the Berlin Wall in 1989. He notes, 'At the beginning of the twenty-first century you cannot base culture on division'.

The NMP team consisted of an interdisciplinary team of urban planners, architects and sociologists from both the Greek and Turkish Cypriot communities. Since 1980 the bi-communal NMP team has conducted their meetings under UNDP supervision in the Ledra Palace, the UN headquarters situated right on the city's Green Line.[9] For both Greek and Turkish Cypriot participants, the project created has a valuable and strategic opportunity to work together. 'Agni' an architect from the Greek Cypriot Municipality of Nicosia, commented: 'All participants were eager to create a common ground for communicating and being creative in their fields, towards not only the creation of a high quality project outcome, but also the establishment of friendship bonds for future co-existence.'[10]

The projected neutrality of the master plan process by the administrating agency, the UNDP, despite its best intentions, could never be fully realized. An architect working with the Northern Cypriot planning office comments:

> Sometimes it is really disappointing when we come together and start to talk. 'Okay, guys, we are the ones really living in bad conditions and without access to the inter-national money, so we need more attention and we are sharing the Old City. You have the resources to undertake rehabilitation, but it is limited on our side. So why don't you be positive and accept that we should get more money than you have?' and they said, 'No, you are 18 per cent and we are the majority, so we have to have more money.[11]

One of the basic aims of the NMP planning was to slow down the degradation of the inner historic city of Nicosia, in fear that 'the heart of Nicosia would soon become a derelict no-mans land' (UNDP 1984: 12). On the Greek Cypriot side of the Buffer Zone, municipal authorities and the mayor were being pressured to assist shopkeep-ers financially with retail outlets along the partition line, which since 1974, had become virtually empty. Planning and financial visions for the Buffer Zone area were not limited to municipal authorities. For example, in June 1991, the Greek Cypriot President, Mr Vassiliou, revealed plans to invest (CYP)10 million pounds via a series of infrastruc-ture developments and financial incentives for rejuvenating property next to the Green Line (Hocknell, 2001). The aim of the assistance was to negate the trend of depopula-tion next to the degraded area and to promote the vision of the city as a reunited one.

For Greek Cypriots, as Hocknell writes: 'the NMP thus complemented the "national struggle" encouraging the breaking down of the nekri zoni [meaning "dead zone" in

Greek] and institutionalizing the possibility of reunification, if not of Cyprus then at least of Nicosia' (Hocknell, 2001: 322).

When the plan was finally launched in 1985, Demetriades[8] celebrated the bi-communal team's work as 'a landmark in the tormented life of our capital city'. Significantly for this research, the primary objective of the NMP was to establish a general planning policy for realistically envisioning the future city of Nicosia in two scenarios: as divided and as reunited. This simultaneous vision of the future city as either together or apart, is perhaps one of the most radical aspects of the plan. It is radical in that it does not automatically assume that a formal peace agreement is a prerequisite for beginning the social and physical reunification process. While the first phase of the NMP's work dealt mainly with providing a macro-planning structure for the city, the second phase of the plan focused on a series of pilot projects, both north and south of the UN Buffer Zone.

The bi-communal sewerage project

> As to sewerage, it is not divided. But if you talk about traffic, it is divided. If you go with your car, you come to a barricade and there is no chance for you to go. It is closed. Some streets are closed because of the war. But for the sewerage, there is no obstacle.[12]

The initial and perhaps less glamorous project that kick-started the bi-communal planning process was a united sanitary sewerage system developed during the five-year period after partition. One of the designer engineers of the sewerage system commented: 'The treatment plant is our baby, and it doesn't have any father or mother … UN, UNDP, US is giving money so we are doing some constructions. It is a world baby; and I am taking care of this baby'.[13]

"From the newspapers: The Municipalities reached agreement on the subject of the sewers of Nicosia". From the Turkish Cypriot Newspaper "Yeni Duzen" of the 28th January 1979.

Figure 5.4
THE BI-COMMUNAL
CO-OPERATION
SEWERAGE PROJECT

The sewerage project was achieved through the swift negotiation skills of Nicosia's two leaders of 1984, Lellos Demetriades and Mustafa Akinci. At that time Nicosia had no central sewerage system. The obvious and urgent reasons provoking the sewerage treatment plant was made clear by Mr Akinci who commented about the project: 'The kidneys were on our side after 1974 and it was not economical nor feasible to build another treatment plant. The Greek Cypriots had to come to an agreement'.[14] Indeed, gravity made the sewerage flow north.

The regeneration of the old town, through the Nicosia master plan process started with small but significant improvements along the Buffer Zone. Similar small-scale initiatives have been spread across the city, creating a series of local public spaces and development projects to enhance the quality of the environment of more recently developed areas. The city has the ability to regenerate housing and public space areas, as it can expropriate former buildings and spaces through the existing Cypriot land tenure system. Beyond the sewerage project, two other special projects activated the Nicosia master plan. To start with, a housing rehabilitation project was built in the Chryaliniotissa area adjacent to the Green Line; and in the northern quarter, the Arab Ahmet area, thirty houses have been restored and neighbouring open spaces have been rejuvenated in the process. The Nicosia master plan has also created thirty-two houses and artisan workshops, and has provided supporting grants to keep families in them. Housing was the first priority in the NMP in attempting social, rather than just economic, revitalization. In contrast to the Solidere development in Beirut, which targets a privileged wealthy minority, Agni Petridou[10] notes that this project was directed towards low- to middle-income groups, 'not targeting [the] bourgeois'. The priority of new infill residential projects was given to young families and the children of previous owners in the old town of Nicosia. A comprehensive incentive policy was put forward by the Greek Cypriot administration made this happen.

As indicated on the map in Figure 5.5, the first phase of the UNDP and Nicosia master plan programme[15] was focused on the two main areas of Nicosia – Omeriye and Selimiye. The second phase is focused on the Phaneromeni and Samanbahce areas. The third phase of the programme is focused on the completion of interventions in Omeriye and/or Phaneromeni areas and the restoration of the Market in the Selimiye quarter. The fourth phase of the programme is focused on Phase 2 of the urban upgrading of Phaneromeni area, and the restoration of Bedestan in the Selimiye area.

Another recent phase (2000–4) of the Nicosia master plan was to undertake a survey of the Buffer Zone in the walled city of Nicosia. The area of the Buffer Zone, which is still under the control of United Nations Peace Keeping Forces (UNFICYP), still divides the historic centre of Nicosia in two parts, running from east to west, through the centre of the walled city. The bi-communal NMP identifies this area as the most important

Figure 5.5

MAP OF THE NEW URBAN REHABILITATION PROJECTS IN SOUTH (GREEK) NICOSIA AND NORTH (TURKISH) NICOSIA

'glue' in the functional integration of the city. Its development was aimed at an overall enriched role for this area, including vital contemporary functions that will bring together people from all the communities of Nicosia, re-establishing this zone as a local interest area in the city.

The Buffer Zone survey made it possible to survey and record the part of the old city of Nicosia that is historically and architecturally very important. The survey came in handy to assist the current political process of opening a checkpoint/crossing across the main shopping precinct, Ledra Street, thus re-establishing the commercial heart of Nicosia. The project also created a useful template for future planning interventions in the area. Additionally, and as importantly, this was a valuable opportunity for Greek and Turkish Cypriot professionals to work together:

> Young professionals, both Greek and Turkish Cypriots, eager to work together and create a common ground for communicating and being creative in their fields, formed the project team. After 11 months of close collaboration, the team members not only managed to produce fine results, but they also established friendship bonds that will hopefully last well into the future.[16]

Collaboration

The case study of Nicosia provides a fertile ground for rethinking the capacity of architects and planners in the post-war city and the opportunity to exploit areas of interdependence and where there is a manifold structural need for collaboration.

Compared with Beirut and Mostar, Nicosia has is farthest removed from the international 'expert' circuit. All the same, it may provide the most positive example for effective co-operative post-war planning and architecture. In this way, the case study provided a clear role for architects as political mediators in the search for peace in Nicosia; as former leader Mustafa Akinci notes:

> My profession helped me a lot in understanding the city, the implications of division. For examples, it helped me a lot in supporting the renovation of the centre of the walled city. Some people wanted huge avenues for the cars ... [This] helped me to understand what a Master Plan means. It helped me to say 'yes' to the challenges and to understand that we are not condemned to stay like we are for the rest of our lives. We must find a compromise to reach a better quality of life on both sides of the wall.[17]

As mentioned earlier, the peace-building process in Nicosia started with a shared sewerage treatment project in 1978, perhaps the least glamorous and most pragmatic approach to professional collaboration possible (between architects and engineers), where both political leaders went on to endorse an exemplary bi-communal master plan. This included progressive recommendations for re-densification, a careful analysis of the bifurcation and duplication of urban functions, an architectural survey of the Buffer Zone, and best-case and worst-case scenario-building, based on actual political contingencies. Despite the success of this joint effort undertaken by Turkish and Greek Cypriot professionals in Nicosia, the political stalemate has still left it largely impossible to implement reform since 1985, as Papadakis (2002: 1–23) comments:

> Both sides are still trying to find a solution – by which they do not mean the same thing – it is not so clear whether they are trying to do this mainly through reconciliation. In any solution, both sides (or large proportions within each side) may then feel that, according to what they consider 'right', too much has been given away and both could end up feeling that a solution has been unjustly imposed on them. One might then wonder how long such a 'solution' will last.

Nicosia thus highlights many possibilities and simultaneous dilemmas, both short term and long term, for ways that architects can become more pivotal in the process of political resolution in the divided city. The Nicosia master plan uses 'scenarios planning' to resolve territorial disputes between conflicting parties. This approach relates to the typologies of Israeli journalist Meron Benvenisti (1982) for post-conflict planning approaches. Benvenisti's 'urban resolver' approach (or the 'equity' or 'urban equalization' approach) is where designers 'engage in constructive intergroup dialogue in circumstances where there are no perceived outsiders' (1982: 27). That is, the approach seeks to achieve the goals of the resolver mode without the problems of imposition.

Other architectural roles being played out in Nicosia include architects as 'pathologists'. One Turkish Cypriot architect[18] commented, for example, on her 'split city' being 'broken-hearted' and said that 'open heart-surgery' was needed in Nicosia's Buffer Zone; for example, a psychiatric centre, or even a recycling facility that could be used by 'both sides'. Consequently, it has become far more important for planners and architects to make small urban incisions (such as the rehabilitation of low-income housing close to the Buffer Zone, identified, for example, in the Nicosia master plan), than to have them developing a fast-track urban rebuilding programme, as in Beirut.

The many challenges of the role of architect as pathologist in Nicosia were revealed in the design studio held there in April 2002, and discussed in Chapter 7. This involved design students excavating and then constructing a coherent picture of the contested city, using architecture as an investigative urban device for starting their design projects. For example, many of the students and local architects involved in the studio suggested that the Buffer Zone would work if you inserted potential commercial functions in it, rather than give it over to political and confrontational uses. 'Pefkios', a conservation architect practising in Nicosia, suggested that the planning solution to reunification lay in the concept of seeing 'the walled city as one unit and one administrative entity to revitalize [the whole]; there is no need to create a Pompeii'.[19]

While the specific example of Cyprus's trajectory of partition is unique in its historic and social background, the opportunity to rethink the future of a bifurcated city through design and planning strategies (prior to a peace agreement being agreed upon) offers critical lessons for architects working upon sites of future ethnic and political division.

Negotiating tools

While there are clear deficiencies in the Nicosia master plan process and product, many valuable lessons can nevertheless be drawn from the project. The fact that the NMP was used for the re-establishment of bi-communal relations in Nicosia suggests that design and planning initiatives can become powerful peace-broking tools for politicians and communities interested in resolving their cultural, ethnic and economic divisions. Many of the Greek and Turkish Cypriot architects interviewed saw clearly that their contribution was as political negotiators in the peace process through the future removal of the Green Line barrier. 'Gul', a town planner from the Turkish Cypriot Nicosia Municipality, comments:

> I am taking part, I will try to help the issue to be solved … they say, 'leave the archi-
> tects out, they don't help.' It's not right. Things are not like this: following separate lines.

You have to go in the pool, see everything, recognize everything, and it's teamwork. It's human, humanity. I love humans; maybe that's the reason.[20]

The success of the master plan process was also contingent upon the strong advocacy role of the two specific leaders in power at the critical and sensitive period of the city's history after 1974, and the strong support of the UN and the EU as project funding agencies. The key to the success and eventual implementation of the master plan process in Nicosia was political and ethnic collaboration. The multidisciplinary team of architects, sociologists, politicians and economists working on strategy confirms that the post-war project should not always be thought of as a purely architectural solution. Rather, there is a need for the assumption of universal values and collective cultural identities to become significant in the peace-broking process. Agni, a local architect in Nicosia comments about the tricky negotiations needed in the bi-communal master plan team:

Architects must keep a low but important profile through collaboration. The common language is English, but also we learnt not to say things that might upset or embarrass the other [Turkish Cypriot] side. The NMP is the only permanent professional collaboration, along with the sewerage project. It is a code; you must be careful. We had to resolve these things at the beginning. But town planning is always a political thing.[21]

The limitations of the master plan for Nicosia relate to many of the problems that were identified (for example, the island mentality) in the previous case study chapter, on Beirut. While the funding of Nicosia's future rebuilding was largely dependent on international development agencies (rather than Beirut's privatized reconstruction), both planning projects deal only with the historic centre of their much larger metropolitan areas.

Figure 5.6
LOW-INCOME HOUSING PROJECT,
NICOSIA, 2000

Pilot projects

The capacity to implement the master plan through a series of bi-communal projects (and the Buffer Zone survey) created a momentum in rejuvenating the formerly dead centre of Nicosia, even before the peace process has been formally launched or substantially negotiated. Economic incentives for former residents and lower-income residents to return to the area adjacent to the Green Line have also been a highly successful component of the original Nicosia master plan project. The funding of the pilot projects, however, depended on considerable support from UNDP and other foreign development agencies. The Nicosia model is, therefore, only possible with large quantities of aid from international development agencies and support from local authorities. This is not always present in other post-war situations, as has been well illustrated in Beirut's privatized reconstruction project, Solidere.

In conclusion, Nicosia provides an alternative design process to the quick-fix economic-generator model of post-war recovery that is much more evident in Mostar and Beirut. Nicosia has highlighted many possibilities and simultaneous, short-term and long-term problems confronting architects and planners who wish to play a more pivotal role in the process of political resolution in post-war reconstruction. The final case study, Mostar, examines another set of reconstruction problems relevant to the role of architects working in war-destroyed cities. Unlike Nicosia, the city is no longer officially divided, but in many ways it maintains the political and social infrastructure of a city that is still more polarized by sectarian and political discord.

Notes

1   Interview with Lellos Demetriades, former Greek Mayor of Nicosia, April 2002.

2   According to Purcell (1969: 270–1, 293) of the 287 Greeks Cypriots killed during 1955–60, sixty died at the hands of Turkish Cypriots, 106 were killed by the security forces and at least 112 by the National Organization of Cypriot Struggle (EOKA) (with a possible maximum of 200), while eighty-four Turkish Cypriots were killed by Greek Cypriots and seven by the British.

3   Interview with Miran Rechter, Program Manager, UNDP Bi-Communal Development Programme, Nicosia, May 2002.

4   The term the 'world's last divided city' was used in *Wallpaper* magazine (Spring 2001) implying that Nicosia is now a fashionable place for tourists who may normally travel to Tuscany or the Dordogne.

5   Conversation with Madeleine Garlick, Civil Affairs Political Officer, United Nations Peace Keeping Forces, UNFICYP, Nicosia, 26 January 2002.

6   Interview with 'George', a Greek Cypriot taxi driver, September 2001.

7   Interview with Lellos Demetriades, former Greek Mayor of Nicosia, April 2002.

8   Interview with Lellos Demetriades, former Greek Mayor of Nicosia, April 2002.

9   The Ledra Palace Hotel inside the Buffer Zone in Nicosia is the primary site where inter-communal meetings facilitated by the United Nations have taken place.

10 Conversation with Agni, architect, Nicosia, April 2002.

11 Interview with Layik, town planner. Nicosia, April 2002.

12 Interview with Nevzat, engineer, Nicosia, May 2001

13 Interview with Nevzat, engineer, Nicosia, May 2001.

14 Quoted from Akinci, *The Cyprus Weekly Magazine*, (1), November 1989: 13.

15 UNDP, US and EU funding made the NMP pilot projects possible.

16 Interview with Nevzat, engineer, Nicosia, May 2001.

17 Interview with Mustafa Akinci, Nicosia, April 2002.

18 Interview with Gul, town planner, North Nicosia, June 2001.

19 Interview with Pefkios, architect, Nicosia, May 2002.

20 Interview with Gul, town planner, North Nicosia, June 2001.

21 Interview with Agni, architect, May 2002.

6

Mostar –
reconstruction as
reconciliation

Figure 6.1
STARI MOST BRIDGE,
PRE-WAR

Thus Mostar joined the ominous club of divided cities (Berlin, Beirut, Nicosia etc.) in which the bridges were replaced by walls. Membership of this club fortunately does not last forever but it is dominated by a political and social rupture of the community that is as traumatic and deep as the physical destruction and human suffering of war. (Plunz, 1998: 78)

This chapter focuses on the case study of Mostar through the theme of design as reconciliation, and analyses the massive exodus of local architects, and reliance on foreign design experts, in the city's reconstruction programme, 1994–2004. Reconciliation remains a simultaneous need and obstacle between the still polarized, post-war Muslim, Serbian and Croatian communities resident in Mostar. The theme of reconciliation is thus critical in any physical and social reunification strategy for Mostar where, ironically, in prewar Yugoslavia, the city was held up as the ideal urban model for ethnic tolerance and co-operation in the (Bosnian region) Republic of Bosnia and Hercegovina.

With the destruction of the city between 1992–96 and its subsequent decade of reconstruction between 1994 and 2004, Mostar is still of great importance in the former Yugoslavia as a symbol of rebuilding an infrastructure of tolerance between ethnic groups. This interest in Mostar is based on the underlying premise that the speedy reconstruction of Bosnia's architectural heritage is a basic requisite to the national healing process across the whole region of former Yugoslavia.

Mostar is also personally significant as my final case study because, as indicated earlier, this is where I first began my post-war reconstruction journey in 1994. My experiences in Bosnia and Hercegovina over the past ten years prompted my subsequent search for other models (Beirut and Nicosia) of successful design processes and projects that may lead to future reunification of divided ethnic territories. Even though Mostar's reconstruction is still largely incomplete, the city still remains a fertile laboratory for developing and testing a framework that might better guide architects working in other cities destroyed by civil conflict.

The experiences of reconstruction in Mostar reflect many of the professional issues faced by architects in Beirut, Nicosia and other ethnically polarized cities such as Jerusalem and Belfast. These include the reliance upon external funding and 'experts', a focus on physical infrastructure and *grands projets*, often with an emphasis on heritage, and, finally, a widespread lack of engagement with local actors and environmental issues in the reconstruction process. For example, in Mostar during 1998–2004, millions of dollars were allocated to the reconstruction of the Stari Most Bridge while the Neretva River flowing beneath contained untreated sewage and hospital waste, making it a public health hazard for the city's residents. During those same years, it was also hard to ignore the fact that only 2 kilometres outside the city of Mostar a growing number of war refugees were living in steel container crates, indicating a profound lack of attention to social reconstruction issues in the city by external agencies.

The lack of a functioning Bosnian state and the nation's consequent dependence on international development aid has created a severely imbalanced national economy and chronic unemployment in Mostar. This makes the small city an unfortunately good example of the faltering socio-political situation throughout much of Bosnia-Hercegovina.

While technically unified under the Dayton Peace Plan (1995), Mostar in 2000 still had two local governments, two universities, two water-supply agencies, two electricity distributors, two chambers of commerce and two municipal bus companies. While much of the official duplication of administrations has since been removed, young local architect 'Senada' recently commented:

> Of course, in Mostar, one boss has to be Croat and the other Bosnian, so in this case, the head of the urban planning department is Croat and the director of the new Urban Institute will be Bosnian and the Mayor is Croat and President of City Council, Bosnian. I can still see on this level a lot of protection of national interests, even though they want to hide it and are always putting some other reasons, but I am afraid that it will always be a problem in urban planning here.[1]

Thus, even though the formal dividing line of war, the Boulevard, was opened after the cessation of conflict in 1994, the bifurcation of the social, economic, political and service infrastructure remains. The multiple reconstruction projects implemented in the city to date have done little to alleviate the perceptions of the Mostarians I interviewed, that Mostar is still, essentially, a politically and ethnically contested city. That is, the promise of reunification remains largely illusory in a city that remains physically shattered and ethnically divided, long after the formal barricade of the Boulevard has gone.

The civil war and Mostar

The background to Mostar's more immediate destruction lies within the complex political breakdown of the former Yugoslav(ia) Federation in 1980 following the death of the President, Josip Broz Tito. The confluence of such internal political factors with an unfavourable external political situation and with the end of the Cold War, led to fierce conflict between different religious groups in the region. The failure of the communist state system can also largely be attributed to the one-party control of Tito's regime and the 'inability of Yugoslavia's economic and political structures to provide economic growth, prosperity and free political expression' (ICG, 1999: 126).

The subsequent unrest across the Balkan region created by the increase of ethnic nationalist movements in the federation, provided the catalyst for eventual and violent takeover by nationalist extremists such as former Serbian President, Slobadan Milosevic, Croatian President, Franjo Tudjman and, finally, Bosnian President, Alija Izetbegovic. The Balkan crisis was also accelerated by the withdrawal of international aid to the federation in the 1980s and the decline of Yugoslavia's importance as a buffer and a meeting ground between East and West. It was a space, according to Kumar (ICG, 1999: 29) which was no longer necessary when Mikhail Gorbachev launched his glasnost and perestroika campaigns.

The outbreak of war in Mostar in 1992, however, was sudden, violent and, for many residents, completely unexpected. As one local resident commented:

> Notwithstanding this, I thought that after 50 years of our kind of socialism, war would never ever recur here. Before this war, if someone tried to convince me otherwise, I would categorically reject even the slightest theoretical possibility of that kind. I thought that brotherhood and unity and equality here were unbreakable.[2]

Following the secession of Slovenia and Croatia, and after a referendum in 1992 favouring Bosnia's secession from Yugoslavia, fierce armed conflict broke out in Mostar on 4 April 1992 between Serbs on one side and Croats and Muslims on the other. A little over a year after the Serbian forces (and population) withdrew, fighting erupted between Croats and Muslims when Hercegovina's Croats established their own para-state, called 'Herceg-Bosna' with its capital in Mostar. With the new state of Bosnia being largely Muslim, the Croatian population sought to establish Mostar as a majority-Croatian city. Muslim residents refused to co-operate with this new state, and for ten months the city was immersed in fierce ethnic combat. According to a report by the World Monuments Fund (2000),[3] over 3000 Mostarians died in the fighting and 60 per cent of Mostar's inhabitants were exiled.

The reasons for the destruction of Mostar are complex and have been analysed by many authors including, Danner (1998), Glenny (1992) and Ignatieff (2003). Bing (2002: 13–16) also describes the destruction of the city's cultural monuments as a mix of ethnic intolerance and a desire for territorial expansion: 'The objective for Serb, and later Croat forces was an aspiration to erase the city's multi-cultured identity. Mostar, like of all Bosnia, was caught between the aggressions of Serbia and Croatia, both harbouring dreams of territorial expansion at the cost of the Muslim population.'

This concept of 'urbicide' (Maiwandi and Fontenot, 2002: 41) as described in Chapter 1 re-emerges in the case study of Mostar. Here, we see a conscious process by its aggressors of urban decimation in the city, with the wilful destruction of buildings, homes and urban infrastructure. John Yarwood, (Director of Reconstruction in Mostar under the post-war EU administration from 1994 to 1998), expands on this concept:

> The architectural manuscript of Mostar expresses an encounter of civilizations, into which the roads from the east and the west, from the north and the south were flowing. Islam and Christianity met here, achieving harmony without imposing it. Thousands of shells were fired into this harmony without imposing it. Thousands of shells were fired into this harmony from all kinds of weapons, a knife cut into it, with one single aim of exterminating the Croatian and Muslim being (Yarwood, 1998: 3).

Before 1992 Mostar was a multi-ethnic and multi-confessional city with the highest percentage of mixed marriages in the former Yugoslavia. The population of Mostar was approximately 29 per cent Croatian, 34 per cent Muslim, 19 per cent Serbian and 15 per cent other (Yugo)slavs. Ironically and tragically, however, at the end of the war, Mostar soon became the most devastated city in Bosnia and Hercegovina and was totally divided along ethnic lines. This division is still anathema to many Mostarians, as one local radio journalist comments: 'From 1566–2000. Mostar was united. Our spirit [could not] be divided, and tolerance was our lifestyle.'[4]

Dividing lines: the Boulevard

When the Austro-Hungarians came here, they pulled the railway through the city, that is, through the area where the Boulevard is located. The railway broke off the Ottoman part, that is, the Old City, from … Austria-Hungary. With this war, that [dividing] line has been revived. To avoid that and to have a unified city it is necessary to liquidate this line.[5]

Running along the western bank of the river, the Boulevard (the Boulevard of the People's Revolution, or Bulevar Narodne Revolucije) marked the front line between the Croatian and Muslim sides in the second stage of the conflict in Mostar (Figure 6.2). The Boulevard has a long lineage as a line of fracture. From Austro-Hungarian rule in 1878, it was the original train line, to its formation as a boulevard in 1967. The Boulevard, like the Green Lines in Beirut and Nicosia, became the major front line for the hostilities that started in 1992 between the ethnic militia groups feuding in Mostar.

The scarred remnants of the Boulevard, framed by torched residential buildings along the former dividing line, still remain, reminding all Mostarians of the wounds of their formerly partitioned city (Figure 6.2). One local resident describes the physical impact of the barrier of the Boulevard during the actual war:

Mili: The division line stretched throughout the Boulevard up to Santic Street. It was huge! I mean, the whole picture of it looked huge, frightening: there were two armies that were divided ideologically and by [sand]bags, as well as by hatred; there were weapons; there were enemies confronting each other…
Esther: And at that time, was there any way at all to cross over that line? Was there any point of crossing?
Mili: Any attempt to cross over the line was awfully risky. Only those who were expelled, mostly from the west side, could cross the line. That is, individuals or groups of people who were expelled were the only people allowed to cross. However, an individual who didn't fall into the mentioned category was not able to cross at all.[6]

A   B

Figure 6.2
MOSTAR'S FORMER WAR FRONTLINE: THE BOULEVARD (A) PRE-1992 AND (B) POST-WAR FIGURE 2000

The destruction of Mostar in 1992 involved the strategic erasure of both cultural monuments and essential urban infrastructure such as urban housing, the water supply and bridges. The former Ottoman section of Mostar's Old Town, Kujundziluk, suffered countless rounds of shelling that tore apart its old bazaar and medieval fortress-like complexes on both sides of the Neretva River. A series of nine bridges were also destroyed, dynamited by the Yugoslav National Army between 24 May and 12 June 1992 and further paralysing east–west access across the city. Apart from the severe loss of its cultural heritage in Mostar, all manufacturing industries in the city and its outskirts were also crippled by the war. In particular, nearly all the grain silos, mills and bakeries were severely damaged by Croatian forces in the second stage of the war in Mostar.

Figure 6.3
DESTROYED INNER-CITY HOUSING, MOSTAR, 1999

The famous iconic architectural monument of Ottoman Turkish rule in the Balkans was the town's Old Bridge, the Stari Most, built in 1556 for Sultan Suleyman the Magnificent by the Ottoman architect, Harjrudin. Historically, the bridge also had the strategic economic and political purpose of solidifying the link between the Ottoman Empire and the hinterland of Ragusa, now Dubrovnik. The bridge survived the fighting for six months. Finally, in November 1993, Bosnian Croat forces shelled the bridge in a highly symbolic and successful attempt to destroy it. Given its deep cultural significance and economic value to Mostar as a tourist destination, Ignatieff (2003: 18) describes this act 'not just a piece of barbarism' but also 'a perverse act of self mutilation'.

Reconstruction without reconciliation

Bosnia after Dayton offered laboratory conditions in which to experiment with reconciliation. Now the money is almost spent and Western governments are heading for the exits. (Ignatieff, 2003: 19)

As well as recovering from war, Bosnia-Hercegovina has also faced the immense task of shifting from a centralized socialist economic system to a dynamic market-based economy. Thus, it faced the need to construct a new legal and institutional framework aimed at the now private-sector, market-led economy, in addition to physical reconstruction and social reconciliation. Thus, in the absence of a functioning economy and systems of local and national governance, urban reconstruction projects in cities such as Mostar have been – and remain – completely dependent on international development agencies. This dependence on international aid has often obfuscated the reconstruction objectives of supposed reunification. For example, West Mostar planner, Darko Minarek, has commented that a 'healthy city [needs] democratic legal processes'.[7] Such democratic processes have been completely absent from the beginning of the reconstruction process, which was led by an EU administration and reconstruction team. Minarek describes how reconciliation and joint planning teams were undermined, albeit unintentionally, by the EU processes:

Darko: When people came from both [the] east and [the] west side, they (we) were immediately physically divided by the table's placement.
Esther: Who did that, the EU?
Darko: Yeah. At the west tables there were sitting people coming from the west side of the city and on the east table there were people from the other side of the city. In the middle, there were sitting the representatives of the EU and UNESCO [United Nations Educational, Scientific, and Cultural Organization].

The EU Administration in Mostar (EUAM) was established after the signing of the Washington Agreement in May 1994. The EUAM had the primary objective of 'reconciling warring parties; building security and creating a unified police force; establishing freedom of movement, holding democratic elections and establishing a city council' (Yarwood, 1998: 12). Since 1995, the agency has spent DM 170 million on repairing 6000 houses, thirty public buildings, twenty-five schools, twenty health buildings, seventy water projects and five bridges.

The leader of the EUAM was the former Mayor of Bremen, Hans Koshnick. Koshnick had wide political powers in attempting the complex task of unifying the city, against many who still saw that reconstructing the city along ethnic lines, like some form of 'cultural apartheid', was still a realistic alternative in Mostar. As one of Koshnick's team commented to Radio Mostar in 1995:

> Their vision is to have two cities here, an eastern part, which is Muslim, and a western part, which is Croat. Sometimes, I think they would even like to build a wall in between. Our vision is completely different. We support the unification of the city. This city was always united with many nationalities here, and we don't think it should be divided.

John Yarwood, a British architect and urban planner, was appointed head of the reconstruction department for the EUAM in 1995. While the EUAM had much success in its immediate repair of the infrastructure, health and civic facilities, its longer-term planning structure was deeply deficient; guided by the expectation that 'every project must be finished and every man should leave Mostar on or before 23 July 1996' (the date when the EUAM mandate ended) (Yarwood, 1998: 25). The same clinical efficiency was displayed in the way the EUAM team focused their reconstruction efforts through what has been elsewhere described as the pathologist approach.

> I came to like Bosnians very much. We were like psychotherapists, helping people to cure their own problem. My colleagues were all good people trapped in a nightmare. Through 1994, I argued that money should not be used like opium (which would breed dependency and subsequent withdrawal shock) but rather as a healing drug, which would leave a strong and sustainable situation after our departure. (Yarwood, 1998: 22)

Barriers to reconstruction

Since the ending of the EUAM, the issue of the co-ordination of urban governance and its lack has been a major problem throughout much of the former Balkan region. The split of national government between three non-co-operating entities (that is, Serbian, Muslim and Croatian factions) has caused a state of virtual political paralysis. This paralysis has made it extremely difficult to establish a viable state, let alone one that inspires any continuing following from its citizens. Indeed, as Ignatieff (2003: 19) argues, 'No small country has more levels of government, more politicians and more possibilities for corruption, extortion or impasse.' This has left a vacuum in which international non-governmental organizations with their own individual priorities, chief of which are to protect the cultural heritage, have often usurped the role of national and local government in policy development and decision-making initiatives.

For example, in 1998 the Aga Khan Historic Cities programme (AKTC) joined the World Monuments Fund to develop a series of 'pilot cultural heritage projects[8] (see Figure 6.4) that revolved around the historic neighbourhoods in Mostar adjacent to the Old Bridge. Included in this programme was the restoration of a number of key monuments, including a series of treasured mosques destroyed during the civil war. Within the framework of a complete master plan for the old city, key historic buildings and open spaces have been restored in close co-operation with the local authorities and residents, attempting to 'reclaim the unique character of this multicultural city' (Bing, 2002: 56). The objective of the pilot projects was to improve the climate for reconciliation among the peoples in Bosnia and Hercegovina through recognition of their common heritage in Mostar. The projects also sought to build local capacity in urban management and to stimulate new job opportunities in an economically depressed area. By helping to reconstruct a national unity symbol (the Old Bridge) and adjoining historic monuments and neighbourhoods, the project represented the first phase of a wider rehabilitation programme. In September 2000 a master plan (developed by the Aga Khan Trust for Culture) was adopted by the city. The plan included an assessment of planning and development problems, a portfolio of fifteen sites in need of immediate assistance, the establishment of a local management office, a training programme for local preservation professionals and the development of a conservation brigade attached to the Preservation Institute to undertake emergency repair work.

Figure 6.4
THE RECONSTRUCTION OF THE STARI MOST BRIDGE PRECINCT (WORLD MONUMENTS FUND AND AGA KHAN TRUST FOR CULTURE)

Misguided priorities?

In terms of rebuilding priorities, much of the reconstruction planning in Mostar since 1996 has focused on rebuilding the Stari Grad (old town). This concentration on cultural heritage and historic city reconstruction as the top priority in Mostar is questionable, according many of the Mostarians I interviewed, given the emergency priorities of economic and social reconstruction. Again, the attitude of many international develop-ment agencies working in Mostar, in seeking to rebuild only the historic core of the city, reflect the problematic concepts of an island mentality and ruin memorabilia outlined above in the chapter on the reconstruction of Beirut. Plunz (1998: 3) comments: 'As for the highly visible problem of rebuilding the historic centre, our position was that its future is dependent on the larger context; and that the technical problems of immediate recon-struction of monuments were already receiving considerable attention.'

However, the rebuilding of the Stari Most Bridge has become central to the recon-struction efforts, especially of international cultural heritage bodies. With funding from the Turkish government, the EU and the World Bank and design expertise from UNESCO, AKTC and the World Monuments Fund (WMF), the stones from the bridge that had sunk to the bottom of the river have been reclaimed. The original Ottoman plans were redrawn and local stone carvers have been trained to rebuild the bridge in the exact same way that Hajrudin (the bridge's architect) did in 1566. The bridge was completed in July 2004.

Approximately US$20 million was spent on the facsimile reconstruction of the Stari Most Bridge, the icon of the prewar city. The strong belief is that, as Calame (2002: 45) suggests, 'the rebuilding of the fallen Old Bridge will heal the wounds of the past by reuniting former antagonists and stitching together a divided city – Christian Croatians on the western side and Muslim Bosnians on the eastern side'. This reconstruction cost was originally estimated at US$10 million (Ignatieff, 2003: 19). In December 2000 stonemasons carved the first stone block to be used in rebuilding the Old Bridge in Mostar. The then Mayor, Safet Orucevic, told reporters, this was a 'symbol of the beginning of coexistence, reconstruction and reconciliation' of Muslims and Croats. The bridge was officially reopened on 24 July 2004.

In evaluating the success of the rebuilding programme therefore, it is critical to note the discrepancy in funding between the amounts allocated for the Stari Most Bridge, namely, cultural heritage projects and environmental projects. That is to say, while there has been no shortage of money to reconstruct the bridge in a historically authentic way, there has been little money set aside – and it has been allocated for use over a ten-year period – to address the problems of the highly polluted Neretva River that runs around and beneath the bridge.

Although the involvement of organizations such as these has been successful in giving Mostar an international profile, they have been widely criticized for not involving local Mostarians in their administrative and political structures, and for the tendency of international aid experts to dominate the reconstruction agenda. Yarwood confirms this in commenting on his experience in Mostar: 'What would be my bottom line? I reminded myself that they had in many ways more knowledge, more insight, and more control over events than we had. Moreover this was their country and their city, whereas I was visitor, here today and gone tomorrow' (Yarwood, 1998: 11).

Economic and social barriers

Another barrier to social reconstruction in Mostar is its high level of unemployment and the lack of economic development projects in the city. Regarding this problem – and the solution – for his city, Bosnian architect Amir notes:

> It's economic. This is the basis for everything. Physically, there is no division. I can go anywhere, to any restaurant. Nobody will take or tell you anything. But I am telling you, they don't have any joint economic projects, they don't have any joint social projects because all the social structure of the city is divided. This is the problem... It is absurd.[9]

Indeed, further intensifying division, the battle for religious supremacy has continued in Mostar through the reconstruction of iconic architectural objects far beyond the official reconstruction programme. For example, just beyond the destroyed Stari Most Bridge on the Croatian side of the former front line, a Franciscan monastery's ridiculously tall clock tower has replaced one damaged in the fighting. While the original clock tower was 30 metres high, the new clock tower is 106 metres tall and overshadows everything in Mostar except for the giant cross the Croats recently erected on a mountaintop overlooking the town. Explaining the seemingly inflammatory nature of such acts, Zijad Demirovic (2001), former Director of the Mostar Preservation Institute, explained that many Croatian leaders in Mostar believe that true reconstruction could only begin by 'giving up the idea of Mostar as the capital of a Croatian Nation'. The cross and the clock tower, as well as rebuilt mosques and minarets in the old Ottoman town, in fact represent a continuation of the war by other means.

Reconstruction to date: an assessment

Given such barriers, it is understandable that limited progress has been made in the physical and social reconstruction of Mostar, in terms of reuniting the eastern (Muslim) and western (Croatian) sectors of the city. The EUAM has rebuilt basic urban services and made many homes habitable in terms of access to water and electricity and repairs to roofing and walls, while projects facilitated by the AKTC have generated a significant network of reconstruction activities for the wider Balkan region. However, few reconstruction projects undertaken to date in Mostar have in any way facilitated design as a reconciliation tool in the larger peace-building process. This assessment is based upon four arguments.

First, all projects resulting from the workshops and consulting agencies such as the Aga Khan Trust for Culture and World Monuments Fund have been projects to conserve individual cultural monuments such as the Stari Most Bridge. However, as Ignatieff (2003: 19) comments, 'Yes people still cross from one side to another. But they still have completely separate lives'. Thus, questions need to be asked about how priorities for reconstructing Mostar were established. For example, how were the most pressing needs for existing and incoming communities living in the city established? Was the reconstruction of Mostar to be treated like a big design problem? Was a conservation and heritage master plan really the solution? Yarwood continues: 'So the reconstruction during the stay of EUAM has never been made meaningful or planned in order to give the citizens a long-term functional city system' (Yarwood, 1998: 8).

Secondly, giving cultural heritage (the protection of cultural monuments) priority over environmental heritage reveals a lack of strategic thinking about the long-term future of the city. For example, little attention has yet to be given to the reconstruction of the most damaged area of the city, the zone of the Boulevard, or to the substantial environmental damage caused by post-war pollution of the Neretva River tributary.

Thirdly, the lack of a long-term employment strategy as part of local capacity-building by international development organizations working in Mostar has critically limited the economic and social benefits of rebuilding actions to date. Former EUAM planner Boris Pulic comments: 'The EUAM should have not become humanitarian organization. Instead it should have invested the money in creating new opportunities for employment and by developing a marketing economy instead of becoming a European experiment and discovery; Mostar has become a European Casablanca and El Dorado' (cited in Yarwood, 1998: 35).

Finally, the domination of international development agencies in all phases of Mostar's reconstruction has limited the capacity of local architects to play a critical role in rebuilding their destroyed city. Additional factors have also hindered involvement of local designers, including the lack of any money with which to pay them from local government during the five or so years after the war ended and that they are still divided by the existing wartime rivalries dominating local agencies. While external funding largely dictated planning priorities, this lack of local involvement can also be attributed to the polarized municipal administration in Mostar. Adding to this lack of co-ordination is still a clear expectation that the autocratic regime of former Yugoslav planning practice (with its reliance on a one-party system) will make decisions through a non-existent centralized state.

While substantial international aid has helped Mostar in the immediate recovery from its savage civil war, the lack of attention by foreign reconstruction agencies to social and economic issues in the wider Bosnian region, has inevitably hindered the development of long-term peace and normality in the city and the wider Balkan region.

Yet, architects are seen as having an important role. As Bosnian architect Amir Pasic suggests, the profession has a much larger role to play (that is, the social reformer role described in Chapter 3) than simply to build buildings: 'He [the architect] is trained to know more in this field than ordinary people. This means that he should come with some light because people are living in a tunnel.'

Interviews with non-architects in Mostar reveal agreement with this point, even if it is expressed in terms of more vernacular concerns. For example, a young resident of the city, Leila, commented: 'So, I think that is very important that role of architects – in that process of reconstruction – is at least to make our environment nicer and normal. It's not normal to have buildings, which are destroyed.'[10]

Lessons learnt

While this study of Mostar has exposed many of the dilemmas of working as an architect in the environs of a post-war city, it has also highlighted the need for design professionals to immerse themselves in the day-to-day realities and professional environment of cities separated by civil conflict and ethnic polarization. With the ongoing exodus of Bosnian professionals, and local urban planning agencies crippled by the war and without substantial budgets, Mostar has become what Calame (2002: 45) terms 'a haven for reconstruction junkies and architects from the outside world'. Along the way, the post-war rehabilitation process has been largely appropriated by foreign donor agencies like the World Bank, the Aga Khan Trust for Culture and the World Monuments Fund. In this way, today in Mostar the persistence of bifurcated municipal planning agencies and weak overall institutional infrastructure still make master planning or consensus-building extremely difficult.

In summary, reflections upon fieldwork undertaken in Mostar include:

1 *The need for immersion.* My limitations as a foreign and temporary observer to Mostar (a ten-day visit once per year) constrained my ability to really understand Mostar's local politics and history. The opportunity in 2000 to actually live and work in one of the three case study cities, Beirut, as elaborated in Chapter 3, facilitated

in this writer a deeper understanding of the root causes of the tragedies of destroyed cities and hence a deeper capacity to empathize with their residents.

2   *The need for public consultation.* While there have been many promises of foreign reconstruction as a catalyst for reconciliation in Mostar's recovery, the main consideration remaining is not so much how to spend millions of dollars, for example on the reconstitution of the Stari Most Bridge, important as this was, but rather the more fundamental challenge of establishing reconciliation through consulting and involving Mostarians in the future form of their city through a process of participatory democracy. That is consultative decision-making which needs consultation with the local community by those who will eventually implement the decision. In this way, architects may play a more substantial role as mediators in the peace-building process and build social as well as physical bridges in healing old wounds of a city severed by religious hostility and destruction. In Mostar while foreign investment and administrative support was needed to compensate for crippled local urban development agencies, the strings attached to imported funds forced priorities upon the city that led to unfortunate results and omissions. At many crucial junctures, decisions were made according to short-term political expediency without reference to long-term impacts, trade-offs, external models or the need for local capacity-building to keep pace with the introduction of new ideas, development schemes and planning tools.

3   *Physical verses political division.* How can architects begin to envisage physical reconciliation when their political system is still divided? The case study of Mostar indicates that the path towards reconciliation can be more effectively facilitated through long-term economic and social planning, than just funding cultural heritage projects, such as the US$20 million spent rebuilding the Stari Most Bridge by foreign donor agencies, most of whom left the city as soon as the bridge was re-erected in 2004. Zimonijic and Tanner comment; 'reuniting the people may prove harder than simply rebuilding the bridge. In many ways the bridge had collapsed between the two largest communities in Mostar long before Croat shells sent the stone blocks crashing into the river' (Zimonijic and Tanner, 2003).

The next chapter seeks to build on the life and research experiences derived from this analysis of Mostar and the previous case studies of Beirut and Nicosia. In it, I review the implications these experiences have for architects working on sites of social conflict and their ability to use design as an effective peace-building tool in the reconstruction process.

Notes

1   E-mail from Senada, architect, Mostar, December 2005.

2   Interview with journalist Marin, Mostar, August 2000.

3 World Monuments Fund report, Spring 2000.

4 Interview with journalist Mili, August 2000, Mostar.

5 Interview with Zijad, August 2000, Mostar.

6 Interview with radio journalist Mili, August 2000, Mostar.

7 Interview with Darko Minarek, architect, August 2000, Mostar.

8 RFE/RL (2000).

9 Interview with Amir, August 2000, Mostar.

10 Interview with Leila, August 2000, Mostar.

7

From Zones of contention to Lines of connection – implications for the design profession

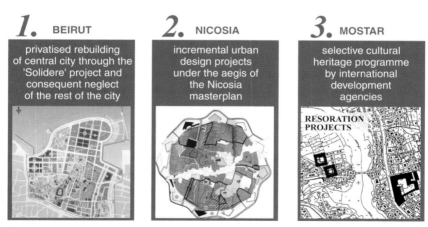

1. BEIRUT
privatised rebuilding of central city through the 'Solidere' project and consequent neglect of the rest of the city

2. NICOSIA
incremental urban design projects under the aegis of the Nicosia masterplan

3. MOSTAR
selective cultural heritage programme by international development agencies

RESORATION PROJECTS

Figure 7.1
CASE STUDY RECONSTRUCTION APPROACHES

People turn to architects for answers. Surely those responsible for shaping structures, those whose discipline has been discussing the comforts, pleasures and mysteries of buildings for thousands of years, could help explain the meaning of this traumatic event. (Wigley, 2002: 69)

This chapter analyses the key themes in the case studies of Beirut, Nicosia and Mostar. The fundamental question driving my examination of the reconstruction in these cities was, how can I, as an architect, contribute to working and researching in urban environments polarized by ethnic, political and social division? The three case studies have illustrated how architects have variously ignored (Beirut), tolerated (Mostar) and almost bridged (Nicosia) the pressing social and physical agendas of reconstruction. New tools are clearly needed for architects to meet the moral imperatives of contributing to peace-building after conflict, not only in the three cases examined in this book but also in present-day reconstruction projects in cities as diverse as Kabul, Baghdad, Jerusalem and Banda Aceh. The chapter begins with an analysis of the key themes emerging from the three reconstruction episodes. This analysis forms the basis of a framework for guiding the contribution of design professionals to the peace-building processes necessary to resolve the multiple physical and social effects of war; that is, a flexible framework for moving from zones of contention to lines of connection. The framework is guided by three 'p' principles: political and ethnic collaboration, public consultation and pilot projects.

The case studies of each of the cities illustrated specific design approaches to tackling post-war reconstruction (see Figure 7.1). These were:

- Beirut's privatized rebuilding of the central city through the Solidere project and consequent neglect of the rest of the city

- Nicosia's incremental urban design projects under the aegis of the Nicosia master plan

- Mostar's selective cultural heritage programme by international development agencies.

Despite these differences in approach, a common and recurring problem has been the priority given to repairing the immediate physical damage over the social and economic priorities of the post-war aftermath. As the studies in previous chapters illustrated, the efforts of many international experts, academics, practitioners and non-governmental organizations in the post-war reconstruction process have been of mixed value. Many architects, planners and conservators arrive in post-war cities essentially as visiting international 'experts' and few are inclined to stay and make any direct and lasting contribution beyond restoring or rebuilding single historic buildings and monuments. In Mostar, for example, Boris Pulic, a local Croatian planner working with the EUAM, commented about the lack of continuity and lasting commitment in the international development community: 'Instead of donating ... fishing rods [to us] and teaching us how to catch fish, we were constantly being donated the ready caught fish'

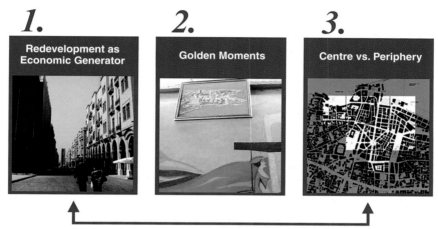

Figure 7.2
KEY CONCERNS IN THE RECONSTRUCTION OF POST-DISASTER CITIES

(cited in Yarwood, 1998: 89). In contrast, Nicosia provided the positive example of exploiting areas of ethnic interdependence, using an infrastructure project (sewerage) as a reconciliatory device, even while the actual legal treaties of peace in Cyprus were still far from resolved.

Three assumptions underpinned the reconstruction efforts in Beirut, Nicosia and Mostar: (i) reconstruction is an economic generator, (ii) that reconstruction should emphasize 'golden moments' from the past and (iii) that reconstruction should privilege the centre over the periphery (Figure 7.2). However, each of these assumptions has been found to be, at best, problematic in all these cities. Indeed, they might be seen as the three concerns central to establishing a more effective practice of reconstruction of war destroyed cities.

Redevelopment as an economic generator

The argument that reconstruction is an economic cure for a country's post-war woes, and therefore a tool of social reconciliation, provided a common rationale for undertaking speedy development projects in all three cities studied. The weakness of the notion that redevelopment can be an economic generator is that the task of rebuilding post-conflict communities is typically carried out as a series of non-integrated and short-term projects funded by donor agencies (Nicosia and Mostar), or by a privatized agency (Beirut). This, as Hasic and Bhandari (2001) note, results in few signs of sustainable growth and often results in failed reconstruction outcomes. It can also accelerate the island mentality to be found in Beirut and widen the socio-economic gap between the haves and the have-nots. For example, urban reconstruction programmes in Nicosia and Mostar have taken little account of new incoming residents whose needs may be vastly different to those of pre-war communities.

Relying on external or private funding sources for reconstruction also often causes an over-dependence on external actors and the neglect of local professionals with a long-term commitment to the social and physical fabric of the city as well as to its economic base. Thus, although Beirut undertook an ambitious privatized reconstruction project under the control of Solidere, economic growth was slow to materialize and the little that might have occurred has been undermined by regional instability. Indeed, by tightly integrating urban reconstruction with the grand economic visions of the state and its associated private-sector alliances, Lebanon made itself vulnerable to the regional instability that was a major cause of its civil war.

In Mostar, reconstruction was originally funded by international development agencies such as the EU and the World Bank. The city now continues to stumble through its tenth year of piecemeal reconstruction as the local economy withers and the promised international funding shrinks to a trickle. Even in Nicosia, whose master plan provided a catalyst for reunification, the area around the Green Line dividing the city has been frozen by third-party interventions monitored by two armies and the UN, and it is still scarred by blight and dereliction on both sides of the interface.

The Beirut model of focusing reconstruction on a sequence of *grand projets* that were hoped to yield good economic returns – either directly or through tourism – has succeeded economically with a sharp rise in regional investment during 2005 in Solidere. At a social level, Nasr (1996: 37) argues, however, that an undue emphasis on 'physically suturing the torn cities' rather than attending to 'socially and economically suturing the torn peoples and above all, to breaking down their mental walls' can never bring peace or economic prosperity. Indeed, in Beirut the reconstruction process has, ironically, both solidified and further accentuated social divisions. Similarly, in Mostar, while millions of dollars have been spent on the reconstruction of individual objects of cultural heritage, most local residents still view their city as essentially divided:

> The city is definitely divided in every respect. This is not so with respect to the phys-
> ical division; that is, there are no movement restrictions… but it is divided in all other
> respects. For instance, there is this division in the city administration. There are six
> municipalities, which are divided between the two sides of the city – three on one
> side of the city and three on the other. Everything is divided, everything is doubled.
> It has never been like that before the war. Mostar is one small city and this doubling
> of services and everything else is ridiculous.[1]

In Beirut the metaphor of a dual city[2] is used as part of the increasing criticism of the Solidere project. Numerous Lebanese architects, planners and journalists interviewed, vehemently objected to the project's concentration on the market of the bourgeois elite, effectively creating an island of financially privileged haves from which the have-nots are banished. In Mostar the division of planning, police and administrative offices across the east (Bosnian) and west (Croatian) precincts continues to preserve and incubate ethnic hostility on either side of the Boulevard, the city's still scarred partition line. In Nicosia, while attempts have been made at bi-communal dialogue between the divided Turkish and Greek Cypriot communities, there is little immediate hope that the divided northern and southern halves of the city will ever be truly reunited on a cultural level.

Golden moments

Memory and forgetting are two sides of the same coin. Indeed, each provides the presupposition for the existence of the other. Remembering everything is as impossible as having no memories at all. (Papadakis, 2001: 4)

A cyclical relationship of memory, deconstruction and reconstruction in the contested terrain of the post-war city is always evident in the rebuilding process. While battles between nostalgia, historicism and modernity were integral to the reconstruction strategies of Beirut, Nicosia and Mostar, all three cities have relied on depicting a 'golden moment' in the life of the prewar city as a device for marketing their own renaissance and repositioning the cities on the regional maps of central Europe and the Middle East.

This iconic nostalgia is represented in all three cities, starting with the myriad postcard images of Martyrs' Square (representing Beirut in the mid-1960s and early 1970s as the city's peak phase). In Solidere's literature (see Figure 7.3). Sarkis describes how 'all manner of nostalgia and sentimentalized recollection were unleashed' in Beirut after the

Figure 7.3
POSTCARD OF BEIRUT, 1965

war with 'hundreds of coffee-table books being published' (Sarkis, 2005: 286). In Mostar the Ottoman Stari Most Bridge is the key emblem for post-war recovery in Bosnia. The issues of spatial memory and amnesia – what we choose to remember and what we choose to forget – through the associated imagery of the rebuilding symbols, are thus pivotal in the reconstruction process.

However, this poses many unanswerable questions. For example, does urban preservation mean restoring Mostar to its prewar condition and effectively creating an open-air museum'? Is the simulation of a souk in the reconstruction of Beirut appropriate for a culture that uses supermarkets? Would not a shopping mall be more relevant, given the decentralization and suburbanization that has occurred in the city over the past two decades? Should we be planning for a reconstructed historic core, or should we pay more attention to the outlying suburban and rural areas of a city? Focusing attention on cultural icons and economic generators, both most often located in the central core of a city, leads to the third error – one that privileges reconstruction of the centre over the periphery.

Centre versus periphery

> First and foremost, what's needed is a comprehensive phased policy to bridge the natural gaps between city and periphery. The periphery should be 'civitasized', not to say civilized, to prevent the 'slumming' of Beirut. (Tueni, 1998: 289)

Many local and foreign architects interviewed in Beirut, Mostar and Nicosia believe that reconstructing the historic core would restore their war-damaged city to its prewar identity and rebuild community spirit. Thus, they rarely focused on the leftover zones, the no man's land; nor did they seem to deem it necessary to consider why cities such as Beirut and Mostar remain psychologically divided along the frontlines of war before they begin working on reconstruction projects. Instead, design professionals often

Figure 7.4
CENTRE VERSUS PERIPHERY:
BEIRUT FIGURE GROUND
MAP, 1990

viewed their key goal as restoring the cultural heritage of the city, especially by preserving centuries-old central city neighbourhoods or iconic buildings or structures.

This concentration of reconstruction efforts in the core of the city, rather than in its areas, has resulted in over-planned historical cores and under-planned regional and metropolitan districts in all three cities studied. For example, many critics of Solidere's work in Beirut argue that the master plan has, in essence, re-created a divided city, divided this time by the area within and beyond the boundary lines of the Solidere development. Similarly, in Mostar, despite many reconstruction projects in the destroyed eastern (Muslim) section of the city, the Boulevard continues to be neglected in planning strategies for the city. Instead, almost all reconstruction efforts since the cessation of war in 1996 have been in the Stari Grad (old town) and the famous bridge, the Stari Most.

This focus on 'cultural heritage' and the ubiquitous 'historic city reconstruction' as the top priority in Mostar is questionable (as it is in Beirut) when the emergency priorities of economic and social rehabilitation in the city and the wider Bosnian state are considered.

In Nicosia, while there has been a strong commitment from independent and public agencies to bring about political change through the tool of the Nicosia master plan, all design efforts to date have concentrated on the historic cores of the Greek and Turkish Cypriot centres. The urban structure of Nicosia, with its different nodes and linear routes, could have formed the basis of a more integrated city with greater variety and intensity of activity across the metropolitan area as a whole. Instead of this, suburban transport provision and connections still need to be improved significantly as suburban sprawl has increased dramatically in outer Nicosia in the past twenty years. The city's existing problems of road congestion, air pollution and social exclusion in residential quarters have only been further intensified through this concentration on Nicosia's urban core rather than its outlying centres.

Towards an operational framework: the three 'p' principles

Many negative lessons for reconstruction are embedded in the application of the three assumptions of post-war reconstruction. However, it is possible to reverse these lessons and see them as guiding principles for an operational framework for architects working on the complex task of reconstructing the physical fabric and reconciling the social life of divided cities. The three key 'p' principles mentioned before – political and ethnic collaboration, public consultation and pilot projects – are central to such a framework (Figure 7.5).

The three 'P' principles

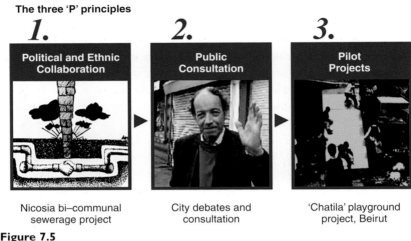

1. **Political and Ethnic Collaboration**

2. **Public Consultation**

3. **Pilot Projects**

Nicosia bi–communal sewerage project

City debates and consultation

'Chatila' playground project, Beirut

Figure 7.5
THE THREE 'P' PRINCIPLES

Political and ethnic collaboration

Achieving political and ethnic collaboration is critical to the success of architects working in post-war cities. However, this demands a radical adjustment of contemporary practice, as it requires architects to consult with non-spatial professionals such as politicians, environmentalists, sociologists, psychiatrists, economists and community representatives when preparing plans for post-conflict reconstruction. For example, the key to the success of the master plan process in Nicosia was that it established political and ethnic collaboration through a bi-communal planning process, and the breakdown of this collaboration was the cause of its eventual limited implementation. However, the original successes of the multi-disciplinary and multi-ethnic team involved in the master plan process shows that reconstruction of divided cities cannot be successful purely in terms of architectural solutions. It is necessary to identify and build in the city a commitment to universal values and collective cultural identities as part of the peace-broking process. The fact that the Nicosia master plan became the negotiating tool for the re-establishment of bi-communal relations in Nicosia shows that design and planning initiatives can themselves be powerful peace-broking tools for politicians and communities interested in resolving their cultural, ethnic, and economic divisions. As 'Pefkios' comments:

> *The basic advantage and the basic value of the master plan was to show that there is a very strong will from both sides to live in a united city. Because Nicosia is an unnatural city, a city that has a wound which has been bleeding for too long. Both sides say, 'How can we stop this bleeding?' At least we agreed on that principle at that time.*[3]

Conversely, there have been few attempts at collaborative planning between the Croatian (west) and Muslim (east) planning agencies in Mostar. This lack of co-operation, together with the stalemate in political reconciliation, largely explains why the city, while no longer technically divided, functions as two separate halves. Similarly, in Beirut, the systemic sectarian bifurcation of all political and development issues and the associated corruption, continues to dominate important reconstruction decisions apart from the privatized *Centre Ville* project.

Public consultation

Public consultation processes are critical to the legitimacy of the planning process, whether just within or just outside a period of war. Wigley comments in relation to the reconstruction of the World Trade Center complex: 'If architects are not used to bringing their doubts about the status of buildings into public discourse, they are unable to contribute to the much needed discussion of architecture's intimate and complex relationship to trauma' (Wigley, 2002: 69).

However, the consultative process is often given lip service by many reconstruction authorities. For example, in Beirut, the public consultation process was limited to occasional public lectures by visiting foreign architects and Solidere exhibitions of design schemes already decided upon and in their implementation stages.[4] In Mostar, consultation on rebuilding projects was limited to international development agencies and the 'experts' undertaking projects in the city rather than with resident Mostarians.

In Nicosia we can see a more consensual reconstruction model where the master plan became the negotiating tool for re-establishing community relations. However, the consultation was limited to 'top-down' situations and, because it lacked broader consensus, it became inflexible. As discussed with many other colleagues reviewing Nicosia's reconstruction, a bottom-up process, which embraces the views of individuals, community groups and local authorities, is critical to developing realizable and sustainable action plans. Such a community-based approach also ensures that residents have a vested interest in the plan's realization and success.

The Nicosia experience suggests that, if sufficient resources are allocated to a long-term reconstruction process, design and planning initiatives can become powerful peace-broking tools which politicians and communities use collectively to resolve cultural, ethnic and economic divisions. None of the three cases investigated in this book, however, comes close to Berlin's consultation model of the Stadtforum. These city debates acted as a kind of public catharsis in promoting comment by Berliners on the future reconstruction of their formerly divided city. As Phillip Meuser, the current director of the Stadtforum, commented:

> *The Stadtforum was initially a planning instrument that brings together planners from the East and the West. I think it's a very important thing because we have the opportunity to bring people from all the parties and groups in society to come together in a round table and discuss ideas and projects without the need for making a decision.*[5]

Gerald Bloomeyer, Berlin architect and one of the initiators of the Stadtforums, expands further on the purpose of the forums by stating that they acted as pressure cookers for letting off steam. He argues that they also had a cleansing role: 'If you allow criticism, you defuse a bomb'.[6]

Public participation in cities destroyed by civil conflict should be structured however, such that there is representation from all sectors of the population, not just the political elites and international 'experts' who control the rebuilding process. This could operate on the basis of either geographical location or special interest, although a framework of robust socio-economic and demographic data is needed for this. Unfortunately, in Beirut, for example, the last official census was taken by the French colonial administration in 1932.[7] In conjunction with public participation, it is thus important to have a comprehensive understanding of the population living and working in specific sectors of the city and what their roles in their communities are and can be. Being able to project who will be the future inhabitants of regenerated areas and how this will affect the demographic profile of a post-war community is also essential. This information is critical to the healthy economic development of the city, as design professionals strive to attain a mixed population in terms of residential tenure and income with the aim of reducing the gap between 'those who have' and 'those who have not'.

Pilot projects

Projects are critical in the implementation of urban planning strategies in post-conflict or natural disaster reconstruction efforts. Without occasionally implementing rebuilding 'plans' how will we know whether the premises upon which they have been conceived have any merit, where they have failed, where they have succeeded? The effort to merge theory with practice in the post-recovery field, however, is a rare phenomenon. This gap is clearly evident in Beirut, Nicosia and Mostar, where an enormous void still exists between the academic critiques of these cities (Hocknell, 2001; Khalaf, 1993; Nasr, 1996; Wise, 1998) and any visible improvement of their physical environments for a wide sector of the population. This situation is not surprising, as to develop major commercial or iconic projects without the collaboration of local professionals would invite criticism. Indeed, the large scale of such projects demands professional criticism.

Unfortunately, such processes detract from the involvement of local design professionals in the reconstruction of their own cities.

The pilot project is defined as a small architectural landscape or engineering project that can be implemented as part of a sequence of long-term rebuilding projects. The pilot project approach is summed up by Oriel Bohigas, one of the key figures in the 1990s renaissance of Barcelona, who comments:

> I believe that this understanding of the city as the sum of its neighbourhoods or identifiable fragments has also been one of the basic criteria in the reconstruction of Barcelona. Controlling the city on the basis of a series of projects rather than uniform general plans makes it possible to give continuity to the urban character, the continuity of relative centralities. (Bohigas, 1999: 32–33)

This type of 'pilot project' was adapted from the set of urban design and architectural interventions executed in Barcelona since 1985 (that is post-Franco), when the city undertook a massive urban rejuvenation programme for the Olympic Games in 1992. At this time in the city, a consensus between the academics and city planners (including Bohigas) guided Barcelona's rejuvenation rather than the generic master plan, which was not seen to be an effective political and spatial tool.

An alternative approach in the reconstruction cycle would be to engage local design professionals and students in small pilot projects. Concentrating on modest projects enables local professionals to test design and reconstruction theories on the ground, if appropriate. Working at such modest scales more easily permits the collaboration of local architects, residents, planners, students and policy-makers than major development works do. Design educators for example, in Mostar, could spend a summer collectively building a simple workshop space for local artisans, or rebuilding a timber deck for bathers and pedestrians on the edge of Mostar's Neretva River. Surely such built outcomes could be more useful than the typical architecture studio process of encouraging foreign architects and planners to fantasize over their drawing boards about structures that would never be built or could benefit the community under investigation? The aim of the pilot project approach is thus to leave something behind, and in this process practically helps to rebuild local capacity.

Despite the seeming paradox, the best example of the pilot project approach observed in the case study cities is the Nicosia master plan. However, this plan was a result of a strong commitment from both the United Nations through UNOPS (1995) and the joint Greek and Turkish Cypriot municipalities to bring about change in the divided capital city, even before a peace settlement had been negotiated. The regeneration of the old town has started with small but significant improvements along the Buffer Zone, including lower-income housing developments in the Greek Cypriot quarter of the city. Similar small-scale initiatives are to be spread across the city, creating a series of local public space and development projects that will enhance the quality of the environment of more recently developed areas.

The pilot project approach works in contrast with the grand designs and enormous budgets of master plans that suit the needs of economic and political elites. Modest and incremental pilot projects were designed to address local quality-of-life concerns. As such, they were small in scale, relatively easy and inexpensive to implement and enabled local people to feel that they had a role in the reconstruction of their built fabric. In Nicosia, for example, the pilot project approach was successfully tested through its master plan, as described above. The malaise however brought on by nearly thirty years of political stasis has often undermined the benefits of these developments.

Finally, while international relief and aid funding may depend on a peace agreement, reconstruction need not wait for the signing of a peace agreement (or the approval of the donor community). Hence, many small-scale initiatives may be possible before the conflict ends. Many barriers to community-based reconstruction are related to the attitudes of the donor community and require an understanding that:

- the dominant relief culture of top-down emergency aid undermines rehabilitation initiatives

- some agencies may be reluctant to transfer control over resources to local communities

- the lack of political will and donor procrastination will undermine sustainable recovery.

To overcome these externally influenced barriers, community-based reconstruction is essentially an exercise in capacity-building. The coping capacities of communities are rarely well researched or understood, and are often underestimated. Thus, there is a need to understand and respect the traditional ways in which communities cope with stress and the skill pool that they can bring to the reconstruction process. There is a need also to build capacity in community participation processes — in both local communities and the international relief community.

Structural barriers to community-based reconstruction often relate to the nature of the post-conflict polity, as well evidenced in the case studies of Beirut and Mostar. Nation states and local authorities may be weak, with newly emerging administrations needing to be built from scratch. Business and land may be controlled by an elite minority at the expense of the majority, the very situation that is often at the heart of the original conflict and which may perpetuate it, especially when post-war economies are structured to favour powerful political actors (for example, as post-war reconstruction in Beirut had for ex-Prime Minister Rafiq Hariri). Despite this, the informal economy is often the most vibrant and responsive to the changed post-conflict circumstances.

However, while the informal sector often represents the most dynamic force in recovery, it is often unregulated and may mask many unmet needs, especially the needs of women. Finally, many of the more intellectual and entrepreneurial sections of the community may have migrated during the conflict and chosen not to return. This leaves a large gap in civil society.

Proactive roles for architects

The challenges I have highlighted in previous chapters relate to the multiple and complex tasks of the architect in improving practice in post-war reconstruction. This involves the process of physically rebuilding war-damaged cities integrated with the simultaneous social reconstruction of their often devastated communities. This section proposes three proactive roles for architects in achieving this, as a positive path forward for design professionals working in zones of conflict: architects as pathologists through the action planning process, architects as social reformers and political mediators, and architects as educators (see also Figure 8.3).

Architects as pathologists

Architects as pathologists have the tools to diagnose the fractured urban condition, analysing and prescribing remedies for dysfunctional and often still politically contested cities. In the diagnostic stage of the divided city, the potential of master plans to effectively control and predict urban growth and form can be scrutinized. Hamdi comments: 'We need to shift our attitudes out of the confines of masterplans, with their singular prescriptive solutions, their reliance of consistency, rather than diversity, with all the futures they envision and the guesswork they entail' (Hamdi, 1996: 13).

Linked to the suggested public consultation process, the action-planning techniques developed by urban planners Hamdi and Goethert (1997) provide a model of consensual planning involving the community and key stakeholders on the sites under investigation. By providing a wide range of stakeholders (rather than just the elected representatives) with the opportunity to participate in the planning process, design can become more comprehensive in its scope and effectiveness than top-down, master plan approaches. A range of action planning techniques, including observation, semi-structured interviews, brainstorming, diagramming, role-plays and group work, are available to ensure that consultation occurs in all sequences of planning and design leading to the end product. However, community consultation without a larger urban design vision at the start of a development may not produce the best results on the ground and can end up in very mediocre architecture and no long-term vision for cities that need rebuilding.

Linked to the concept of architect as pathologist is the 'restitching' of the torn urban fabric. This strategy is what many architects commonly assume is the most appropriate reconciliation and rebuilding strategy in post-war centres. For example, in the Sahat Al-Borj (Martyrs' Square) reconstruction in central Beirut, the original aim of Solidere, according to local architect, 'Robert',[8] was to 'delete the area of conflict and attempt to produce a coherent public space for all sides'. This aim was never put into practice. In Nicosia many of the students and local planners and architects interviewed as part of this research suggested that the Buffer Zone (the area between the dividing lines of its Green Line) would work if you inserted (like a shish kebab) potential commercial functions rather than political and confrontational uses. 'Pefkios', a conservation architect practicing in Nicosia, suggested that the planning solution to reunification lay within the concept of seeing 'the walled city as one unit;[9] whereas in Mostar, there is little evidence of the will of architects and policy-makers working on the rehabilitation of the city to reconnect the formerly severed city.

The idea that the role of the architect is that of a pathologist was integral to the three design studios held in Beirut, Mostar and Nicosia (see Chapter 8). This diagnostic approach was developed to prompt students to react to the given site with an initial design reaction that they could then further test through consultation and site analysis. Again, there are clear limitations in expecting that the results of a series of interviews and surveys and opportunities and constraints analysis can be spatially transformed into an innovative and site-responsive design proposal. On the other hand, without an analysis of the dysfunctional city by consultative methods, superficial and short-term design solutions are likely to materialize, as is well evidenced in Beirut and Mostar.

The desire to reconnect the east and the west sectors of Mostar, Beirut and Nicosia was a popular strategy tested through all the 'Dividing Line' studios described in the next chapter. Architecture and urban design students appeared to believe that the restitching strategy could have a direct impact upon reconnecting severed post-war communities.

Architects as social reformers and political mediators

Can architects be socially responsible and inspire a collective and collaborative discourse in the spatial and political processes of reunification? While the restricted practices and theories of the profession have reduced the scope of architecture to what Crawford

(1991: 43) terms 'two equally uncompromising polarities: compromised practice or esoteric philosophies of inaction', there is still the opportunity for architects to work more effectively as social reformers and political mediators. In Beirut, for example, architects such as Assem Salaam and Jad Tabet were immediately vocal in their opposition to the Solidere reconstruction plans after the war in 1991. Between 1994 and 2004, however, there has been little public protest, civic activism or even calls from the profession for transparency in the privatized reconstruction processes. Through their silence, architects in Beirut (as suggested by many of the interviews with Beiruti residents) become accomplices in a reconstruction process that excludes any level of social reform.

In Mostar, many local architects interviewed claimed that they had little chance to contribute to the reconstruction agendas of the international development agencies. However, local architects in Nicosia were successful political negotiators within the framework established through the Nicosia master plan by UNOPS. In proposing lower income residential housing as part of the master plan in inner-city Nicosia, social reform has been attempted as part of a slow but equitable reconstruction process. Their simultaneous vision of the future city as one in which they will be either together or apart is one of the most radical aspects of the Nicosia plan, radical in the sense of waiting for a formal peace agreement before beginning the social and physical reunification process.

My investigations have led me to believe that the design profession must learn to collaborate with other disciplines involved in rebuilding societies after sustained conflict, if architects are to move towards the role of social reformers and political mediators. In such a scenario, lawyers, economists, planners, architects and sociologists (both local and foreign) could work with local residents and politicians to formulate strategic processes for re-activating peace across a long time span. This is not to say that mistakes and misunderstandings would not occur along such a multi-professional path, but a visionary framework established at the outset of such a collaboration could be hoped to guide the peace-building process to a more equitable outcome.

Architects as educators

Architects as educators have two main tasks. First, when teaching design, planning and conservation in academic institutions, architects have a moral duty to use the design process to investigate the acceleration of environmental and war-damaged sites. This requires the revision of, and logistical support for, many architectural programmes in many countries struggling with developing professional higher education programmes. The second task lies in educating the public about design, its process and its consequences. This sequence also needs to be applied in reverse, with architects learning from their public constituency in the process of consultation on proposed rebuilding projects.

The three Dividing Line design studios discussed in the following chapter were used as a laboratory for deliberating upon effective reconstruction processes and design speculations for Beirut, Mostar and Nicosia. The analysis undertaken in the design studios attempted to re-envision the object-based and historic city formulae of the work of traditional architecture studios towards generating schemes that envisaged a long-term approach to reconstruction. For example, most of the 'It is about time' studio projects developed for Nicosia suggested a range of design proposals that could be implemented over one to ten years, depending on the sequence of peace initiatives that are hoped to eventuate in Cyprus in the next few years.

The impact of the Dividing Line studios upon young architects and urban designers was an extremely positive outcome of my original fieldwork. My aim had been to empower young architects in considering their own social accountability in their role as urban arbiters. In many of the studio exercises, students were challenged by basic questions of 'what is right and what is wrong' when dealing with complex urban sites and associated social conflicts. One Beirut student remarked:[10]

> I do think that the role of the architect in the post-war field is quite controversial: he/she must acknowledge that it is not within his/her power to stop conflict and establish reunification. Actually I think it is easier for architecture to divide rather than unite: division being more rooted in people's behaviour.[11]

Again, Garry Ormston (University of Melbourne graduate urban design student) commented thus about his experience in Mostar: 'Obviously there is a role for immediate emergency relief, for architects anyway. For me, though, it is really a more long-term role, getting the debates going about the future, making the contacts on all sides, identifying projects that will help engender a pride in the community once again.

Similarly, young Beirut architecture students who visited the neighbouring island of Cyprus as part of the 'It is about time' studio (April 2002) were overwhelmed by the opportunity to work on another city, apparently 'more divided' than their own. As a female design educator working in the domain of typically male profession, I have also tried to introduce some level of anthropological analysis of women's views and roles in the case study cities. I attempted this by asking students to undertake semi-structured interviews with marginalized actors in reconstruction, such as women and children, as their initial site-analysis.[12] I have found that this type of analysis provides intense insights into the social and physical experience of living in a city partitioned by ethnic conflict. This qualitative or ethnographic examination of women's lives in the design process reveals what Sophie Watson describes as understanding some of the 'more subtle ways in which gender inequalities have a nasty habit of tenaciously persisting' (Watson and Gibson, 1995: 256).

Mobilization

Bringing down walls, both in fact and symbolically, is a major contribution of architecture to the promotion of human rights. As this example shows, both real and symbolic walls are relevant to architecture and ethics. (Perez-Gomez, 1983: 73)

The case studies indicate that urban planners, architects and conservationists have tended to avoid direct intervention in urban centres destroyed by conflict. With the current epidemic of natural and manmade disasters, from 9/11 to the 2004 Boxing Day tsunami and beyond, design professionals can no longer remain blind to the presence of socially dysfunctional and environmentally fragile cities. Further, analysis of the post-war terrain across Beirut, Nicosia and Mostar, also suggest that the orthodox tools of urban planning employed after the Second World War (for example, the master plan approach) are questionable when you have neither a definable political authority nor an investment structure in place in the city that is to be rebuilt. I propose, therefore, that small incremental pilot projects may be more appropriate models in stimulating investment and reconstruction within and outside urban centres disrupted by war.

The design studios described in Chapter 8 tested a multidisciplinary approach to the reconstruction process by engaging in an action planning process with invited sociologists, historians, lawyers and urban activists. Typical design analysis phases were supplemented with qualitative research methods, such as conducting interviews and public workshops in the divided cities under investigation. The role of architects in these studios was more that of the mediator and facilitator than the stereotypical design hero outlined in Chapter 2, reflecting the collaborative processes used by Nicosia master plan team. The success of this process and the design studios suggests that this approach offers a repeatable model for designers working in future post-conflict environments.

One key element of this model includes mobilizing architects as key participants and urban mediators in the larger peace-building process in post-war reconstruction. My research into the capacity of architects working in cities polarized by ethnic conflict suggests that design professionals can be very active participants in the peace-building process after war. In a similar way, architects could metaphorically spread their professional wings to envisage using their creative and negotiation skills to deal with the urban symptoms of ethnic rivalries and the associated urban malaise common to the post-war city.

Conclusion

Many architects and urban policy-makers working in the aftermath of civil conflict interviewed during my visits to other post-war cities, including Jerusalem and Belfast, suggested that little can be done in reconstruction planning until the political situation is clarified and settled. In light of this stasis, architects need to find other ways to work in the post-war context; ways that are not aloof, passive or deferential, or confrontational. More research is needed to observe the patterns that lead to civil violence and displacement, and to look at how this is manifested in the physical domain. Is it possible to design clever buffers, remedies or release valves in order to mitigate the worst effects of the negative changes, assuming we cannot stop them altogether?

One example ripe for further examination is Belfast. As the peace-line walls continue to be built in that city, can architects and planners begin to adjust that process – so that public consultation mechanisms involving design can be put in place, aiming at providing future common ground between those who are currently engaged in making barriers? In relation to racial divides in New Orleans, Louisiana, Calame (2002: 45) suggested ways to tackle these challenges in a more pre-emptive way: 'In a racially divided city you could imagine taking on de-densification projects grounded in low-income housing rehabilitation that would distribute segregated black populations into segregated white neighbourhoods.' The research question emerging here for future investigators is, how can architects engage in what Benvenisti (1982) describes as the problem-sharing processes needed in urban centres such as Belfast, Jerusalem and New Orleans, broken by systemic urban conflict? Is it our role to provide the definitive solution, or rather to provoke an open-ended process of interaction that can inspire collective action in rebuilding civil society after the disaster of war?

Concentrating on emergency repair efforts and associated 'fast-track' development projects was a common problem dictating the reconstruction programmes of Beirut, Nicosia and Mostar. In Beirut, for example, except for immediate infrastructure and building repair in the *Centre Ville* area (including the airport and connection road to the central business district in 1993), the city is still undergoing very slow piecemeal reconstruction by building-owners, fourteen years after the civil war ended in 1991. Metropolitan areas directly outside Beirut that were affected by the war, (for example, the northern city of Tripoli and the southern Beirut suburb of Ouzai) have been left behind in the race to rebuild the city's heart – the new privatized Solidere precinct, sited within the city's former downtown area.

In Nicosia, the United Nations authorities that still control the area have maintained the Green Line (or Buffer Zone area) as a crumbling museum piece. Despite limited housing rehabilitation in the city, the pilot project initiatives of the Nicosia master plan have mainly concentrated on restoring cultural heritage icons in the northern and southern sides of the still divided capital city of Cyprus.

In Mostar, where my post-war cities trek first began in 1994, the severe limitations of a divided municipal administration have resulted in the lasting intervention of foreign professionals in all types of reconstruction planning and projects. Because of its significance as a symbol, a priority for both local leaders and outsiders was the repair and reconstruction of the badly damaged historic core (Stari Grad) and its famous and iconic Ottoman bridge, the Stari Most. Making Mostar's cultural heritage the top priority has thus limited the impact of reconstruction on the more pressing agendas of chronic levels of unemployment and sectarian divisions in the city.

Faced by the immense and complex challenge of working effectively in the post-war environment, how can the architect again become a crucial figure in the remaking of a profession that looks more towards humanity and social justice than singular objects and related profit? The final chapter speculates how design educators can refocus the profession upon social and ethical concerns and can contribute to the reconstruction of the proliferating group of cities polarized by ethnic and economic conflict.

Notes

1   Interview with Mili, June 2000.

2   The term 'dual city' is used by Peter Marcuse to describe the ancient device of creating boundaries reflected in social and physical walls. 'Cities today,' he writes, 'seem fragmented, partitioned at the extreme, almost drawn and quartered, painfully pulled apart' (1999: 170).

3   Interview with Pefkios, Nicosia, April 2001.

4   For examples of the exhibition of the 'Souks Competition' and 'Gardens of Forgiveness' project refer <http: //www.solidere.com.lb>.

5   Interview with Phillip Meuser, Stadtforum convenor, 10 October 2001, Berlin.

6   Interview with Gerald Bloomeyer, architect and publicist, 23 February 2001, Berlin.

7   See <www.country-studies.com/lebanon/population.html>.

8   Interview Robert, architect, June 2000, Beirut.

9   Interview with Pefkios, May 2002, Nicosia.

10   From a term paper by architecture student Celina Akar in the 'Divided-City' seminar, American University of Beirut, May 2000.

11 Studio feedback report, Garry Ormston, Melbourne University Mostar Studio, June 1998.

12 Interviews with local people conducted by AUB architecture students in 2000 in their Green Line projects gave them great insights into the real needs of their immediate neighbourhood spaces.

8

Architects without frontiers – implications for design education

We focus on edifice, but architecture itself is whatever percolates out of our activity as trained architects. Invitations are everywhere for us to step back out into a broad section of society, if we would show a willingness to reinvent ourselves and allow the profession to percolate one again. (Scott-Ball, 2004: 135)

The previous chapter analysed the assumptions that underpinned the approaches to reconstruction adopted in the three case study cities of Beirut, Mostar and Nicosia, and turned them around to propose a flexible framework for an alternative approach to professional practice in the post-disaster field. This approach combined community-based design and pilot projects in such a way that the reconstruction of the physical fabric of the city became a peace-building tool by integrating and promoting social and inter-ethnic co-operation. One important dimension of this alternative approach was the expansion of architectural and design education to encompass a critical engagement with the ethical issues of social responsibility and commitment in professional practice. As Wigley (2002) suggests, with little sense of the political implications of their work, many in the design profession are locked in a moral void, willing 'to work anywhere for anyone', moral, social and environmental values notwithstanding. This chapter expands that view through descriptions of three design studios that were undertaken with students, one in each of the three case study cities.

In seeking a way to inspire young architects and urban designers to become more socially engaged, I conducted three Dividing Line design studios (1998–2002) in Beirut, Nicosia and Mostar. All the studios were based on two of Peter Rowe's concepts for design education – 'actionable knowledge' and 'lifecycle learning'. Rowe describes actionable knowledge as a key dimension of the design studio in which the definitions of design problems are at once a guide to solutions and an influence in themselves on redefining the problem and future outcomes (Rowe, 2002: 25). Rowe's second concept, lifecycle learning, is also embedded in the studio process as a means of simulating the decision-making processes common in a professional design office, as well as drawing upon the rich experiences of 'seasoned practitioners as participants in their own mid-career and continuing educational settings, alongside of neophytes in the field' (Rowe, 2002: 28).

Apart from the educational benefits to the students, the aim of the Dividing Line studios was to generate alternative visions of the future of the three case study cities to those being proposed by the dominant decision-making processes of government or private reconstruction agencies. To address the lack of public engagement in the rebuilding process, each of the studios involved a lengthy consultation process with local architects, planners and residents to assess the nature and direction of future design work in the city.

The design studios also used structured interviews to provoke discussion about the realities of living in post-war cities and the roles of architects in their future peace-making. In all three cities students worked collaboratively in small groups to analyse the site, conduct the interviews, develop their design and submit the final project. The assumption was that architecture students could use their design education to transcend the barriers of culture, space and social prejudice manifested by, for example, young Beirutis who were still affected by the historical tragedy of the 1975–91 civil war that had dominated their childhoods.

The Dividing Line design studio process also revealed much dissatisfaction with the direction, focus and pace of traditional approaches to design-studio based learning and enabled the characteristics of alternative design approaches to be explored. While teaching courses can be developed to impart design skills, formulating a pedagogy for architects based on ethics and encouraging students to contribute practically to social change, is much more difficult.

One of these more practical approaches built into the studios I conducted was introducing the concept of pilot projects, (as discussed in Chapter 7), that is, 'walking the talk' and seeking to implement a small component of a larger design studio scheme. The pilot project model was developed through both the Melbourne University Mostar studio I organized in 1998 and the Demarcating Lines studio in Beirut in 2000. For example, in Beirut one of the students built a children's playground in the overcrowded Palestinian camp, Chatilla, as part of his semester's design work. In the Mostar studio, two post-graduate urban design students initiated the 'East–West Connection Project'. The 'East–West Strategy' aimed to reconnect the still largely severed city of Mostar through a series of landscaping and urban design improvements, now under consideration by local authorities in Mostar, eight years after the studio was completed.

The Dividing Line studios were thus a strategy for helping young architects see design as very much part of the overall reconstruction process. Encouraging students to be open to this process and improving their awareness of cities divided by social and ethnic discord was made explicit in lectures and projects I devised during the studio process. The purpose of this knowledge transfer through design was to empower students to develop their own long-term design philosophy, to become more effective at explaining their projects to a non-architectural audience and, finally, to enlarge their architectural careers as future mediators, peace-builders and, eventually, educators.

Studio processes

In design studio and seminar courses organized between 1998 and 2002 (Figure 8.1), students developed solutions and theoretical approaches to specific war-damaged sites and then defended those solutions to juries of peers, experts and representatives from the city they were examining. The studio process I conducted was based on Hamdi's assertion that learning 'can be best generated if education takes the form of debates and practice based rather than theory-led pedagogy' (Hamdi, 1996: 111). For example, in April 2002, the former Mayor of Nicosia, Lellos Demetriades (also a catalyst for the Nicosia

1. MOSTAR

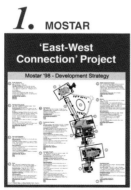

Melbourne University 1998

2. BEIRUT

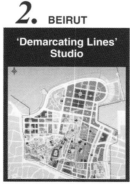

American University
of Beirut, 2000

3. NICOSIA

American University
of Beirut, 2002

Figure 8.1
THE DIVIDING LINE DESIGN STUDIOS

FACILITATOR

- Explain trajectory of post-disaster city condition through historical and spatial analysis of case studies.
- Frame problematic of post-disaster city under investigation and relevant design problem solving methods.
- Construct research and design methodology for studio process ie. site analysis, interviews etc.
- Evaluate design projects in their response to city under investigation.

STUDENTS

- React to current post-disaster city condition.
- Frame a theoretical position from on-site visit and political and cultural context in which the studio process is taking place.
- Develop design alternatives, speculations for peer and case study city review.

Figure 8.2
THE ROLE OF THE FACILITATOR AND STUDENTS

master plan) contributed in the final review of the students' work. The great pedagogic value of the design studio process is that students were required to 'make predictions, think divergently and convergently, apply values, make decisions, argue, work with other people, present ideas and defend them' (Lang, 1997: 123). My role in the design studio process was similar to the conductor in an orchestra – setting the framework, pace and tone of the problem under investigation. The roles of architecture students and the design studio facilitator are outlined in Figure 8.2.

Dividing Line studio I: The Boulevard studio, Mostar, 1998

Alternatives for Mostar's reconstruction were investigated in a design studio project conducted for University of Melbourne design students in 1998.[1] The aim of the Boulevard studio was to explore alternative roles for architects in the Mostar reconstruction process by identifying design principles and proposals that could enhance social integration and support the volatile peace process in Mostar that was well under way when the studio was being held in 1998. The primary objectives of the University of Melbourne studio were thus to provide realizable design concepts that could enhance the future reconciliation of the divided city. This contrasted with other international design workshops held in Mostar at that time that had concentrated less on reconciliation as a strategy and more on rebuilding the historic core of the city. Indeed, numerous heroic schemes for reconstructed and deconstructed versions of the Stari Most Bridge had emerged during many such workshops, with student projects detailing postmodern glass and steel reconstruction projects for replacement bridges and expensive heritage reconstruction. While such schemes were being theorized and laboured over by foreign academics and their students, the city in many locations still had limited water, sanitation and basic housing for displaced refugees and returning Mostarians.

In co-ordinating the Mostar studio we believed that a co-ordinated and sensitive approach to social and physical reconstruction was needed. The following strategies were employed in structuring the 1998 project:

- Collaborating with local architects, planners and residents in assessing the need for future design work in the city.

- Using the design process to provoke discussion. Students arrived in Mostar with some preliminary design concepts to test on-site, rather than assuming that the actual site visit was the point at which to start designing.

- Setting students to work collaboratively in groups for site analysis and for the final project submissions that, together, presented a vision for the whole Mostar region, rather than focusing on individual sites and design concepts.

The studio was conducted as part of the Mostar 2004 (1997–2003) series of international design workshops, co-organized and funded by the Research Centre for Islamic History, Art and Culture in Istanbul and led by Amir Pasic, an architect from Mostar who was forced to flee when fighting broke out in the city. Collaborating partners also included the Aga Khan Trust for Culture, the World Bank, the World Monuments Fund, UNESCO, the Inter-University Centre in Dubrovnik, the University of Sarajevo and the University of Zagreb. Throughout the post-war reconstruction of Mostar, the Mostar 2004 programme provided an annual forum for ideas and involved more than 500 scholars, students and professionals from twenty-five universities in fifteen countries.

The Mostar 2004 workshop series emerged as a strategic professional forum where scholars, students and professionals met, exchanged ideas and co-ordinated the development of new practical rebuilding proposals. The solutions developed have proved to be applicable to many other historic urban centres in the Balkans and have a wide relevance to the fields of architecture, planning and preservation in the general rebuilding process. For example, the eighth annual workshop in 2002 was organized in the form of the summer school and involved graduate and diploma students from seventeen universities and their professors. In order to generate comments and proposals of the greatest relevance to ongoing reconstruction and development activities in Mostar, the participants focused on key urban and architectural sites and concerns facing the municipality, including the interpretation of the architectural fabric, economically viable restoration, design in context and utilizing global communications to support the revitalization effort.

The Boulevard studio process

After an initial analysis of the existing reconstruction reports, city maps and tentative reconstruction plans from local government agencies in Mostar, the student group investigated a range of sites, including broken bridges and the ruins of the university in eastern Mostar which was built during the war on the site of the former army barracks. The aim of the workshop was to work with the city's reconstruction agency (which had fifty-three staff before the war but a staff of only three in 1998, and two of these were about to retire) with concrete and feasible proposals for the reconstruction of critical civic institutions and destroyed landscapes and infrastructure (Figure 8.3). One of the projects, for example, focused upon the rehabilitation of Mostar's Neretva River.

ARCHITECTS AS . . .		CONCEPT	DESIGN STRATEGY
	 PATHOLOGISTS	Architects as diagnosers of the divided city condition. Small 'incisions' designed to help city recuperate slowly.	Actions plans.
	 SOCIAL REFORMERS & POLITICAL MEDIATORS	Peace builders within larger political framework.	Public Consultation.
	 EDUCATORS	Influencing curriculum via introduction of damaged sites into the design studio process.	Academic workshops and 'knowledge transfer'.

Figure 8.3
ARCHITECTS CAN TAKE A PROACTIVE ROLE IN REBUILDING WAR-DAMAGED CITIES.

The 'East–West strategy'

I would also liquidate the historic division. How? I don't know. Perhaps through an international competition. I would make such a programme under which a half of the Boulevard, half of the division line would disappear, under which the 'Berlin Wall' would be erased.[2]

Many architectural schemes were developed from the 1998 Melbourne University studio, including proposals for childcare centres, libraries and community centres. Most of these projects focused upon the social needs that were identified in discussions with local community groups and planners. One of the most modest proposals was the

'East–West strategy' by Beau Beza and Garry Ormston. This scheme was directed at reconnecting Mostar across the river and the Boulevard, via small-scale urban design improvements of improving the riverbank promenade and rehabilitating cultural institutions such as libraries along the main east-west axis.

As discussed in Chapter 5, the Boulevard still psychologically separates the Bosnian (Muslim) and Croatian (Christian) sides of the city, even though access is technically possible. The 'East–West strategy' thus proposed an incremental sequence of landscape, cultural, educational and multimedia renovation projects. Most significantly, it also aimed to re-establish a meeting ground for the still largely divided resident population groups of Bosnian and Croatian Mostarians. Thus, the project sought to address the lack of reconnection and reconciliation projects in Mostar.

The 'River of Light' project developed from the original East–West studio project and was based upon the framework of principles for architects working in war-divided cities that emerged from the case studies of Beirut and Nicosia and recontextualized to the historical, social and political situation in Mostar. Thus, where the EUAM team focused on the immediate rehabilitation of urban infrastructure, the 'River of Light' project had a longer-term urban design and environmental focus. Where projects by international agencies such as the Aga Khan Trust for Culture, the World Bank, the World Monuments Fund and UNESCO focused on heritage conservation projects, albeit in the name of restoring inter-ethnic harmony, the River of Light project focused directly on the need for reconnection and sought to give it physical form.

Where other Mostar 2004 workshop proposals focused upon refining elements of a master plan for Mostar, this project was based on small-scale incremental interventions. The River of Light project respected heritage concerns but added to them a concern for the quality of life and environment of people living in Mostar today. And where almost all reconstruction work has been based upon top-down often externally driven decision-making, the project is based upon extensive collaboration with all stakeholders, especially the staff in local authorities and local people. This collaboration assisted in understanding that most of Mostar's residents still saw their river and access to it as an important reconstruction priority. Community awareness of the project was enhanced by artistic installations along the east–west line during the 8th Mostar workshop in July 2002. These served as symbols of the extensive lighting programme for the east–west axis of the city envisaged as a River of Light.

The overall strategy of this concept allowed for the gradual development of the space as the project resources allowed. A key phase of the project was to tackle the degraded environment of the Neretva River by a series of modest projects to address point-of-source pollution. One of the worst casualties of any war is the environment.

Currently, overflows of untreated sewage and hospital waste flow directly into the Neretva River, severely limiting its recreational use for the city. The Mostar authorities and international agencies were discussing a US$20 million project to upgrade wastewater treatment in Mostar, but no timelines had been developed or funds allocated for it.

Ten years after the formal end of hostilities in Mostar, small urban gestures such as the modest River of Light project were aimed at provoking the people of Mostar to view their city in a new light. It was important, therefore, in the reconstruction process to suggest urban design improvements that most functional cities put in place as a matter of course. This happens in many ways – from rubbish bins and street furniture at the very smallest scale, to major public space, parkland and infrastructure redevelopments. Again, improved lighting and pedestrian passages, as in the River of Light, is just one way which, if implemented, could make an important contribution, given that the people of Mostar traditionally promenade through the streets in the evening. It might change their experience and perception of the promenade, and encourage them to think about the urban redevelopment of their city in wider terms than just housing and rebuilding religious monuments. While we are still unsure of the final implementation of the River of Light (owing to limited funding opportunities), the process has attempted to initiate small-scale, incremental rehabilitation projects involving the original students in the scheme, with strong involvement of local actors.

Dividing Line studio II: Demarcating Spaces, Beirut 2000

How do we gauge the ideas and aspirations of young Beiruti architects? Between 2000 and 2002, I co-ordinated a series of design studio projects as a Visiting Professor at the American University of Beirut. It is ironic that in Beirut there are nine Departments of

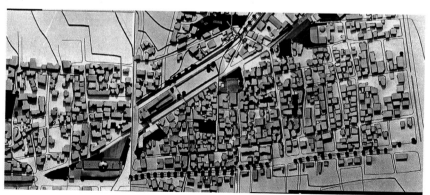

Figure 8.4
DEMARCATING SPACES PROJECT MODEL, BEIRUT 2000

Architecture and, in a city of only 2.5 million people, approximately 6000 graduate architects. Yet, as any observer might question, what has been the impact of this design education on a large number of young Beiruti's and on the recent developments in Beirut and its periphery that have been built since the end of the civil war?

As in the Mostar Dividing Line studio, the Beirut studio was designed to enable students to explore alternative roles for architects in the reconstruction process to those being proposed by architects working on the Solidere project. The studio involved both undergraduate and master's students moving between design speculations, public consultations and testing proposals on-site. The theme of 'Demarcating Spaces' referred to using design to dissolve metaphorically the dividing barrier of Beirut's Green Line. This zone was used as an academic laboratory for examining the current status of physical division and social conflict in the city. The studio was preceded by a series of seminars that explored current theories of post-war reconstruction and the role of designers working in cities after conflict. The course investigated case studies of design strategies for five war-divided cities: Berlin, Mostar, Nicosia, Belfast, Jerusalem and Beirut. My aim in exploring this range of case studies was to encourage Lebanese students to think beyond Beirut and their own personal experiences and to analyse geopolitical theories of reconstruction. The seminar series concluded with each student presenting a one-page divided city manifesto, in which they clarified their personal beliefs about the purposes of reconstruction and their responsibilities as future architects.

Several common themes permeated these manifestos. The first was the recognition of the limitations of the privatized reconstruction model followed by Solidere. While they recognized the importance of safeguarding their cultural heritage and the role it can play, at least theoretically, in rebuilding national identity and prosperity, they also recognized the special responsibilities of design professionals to be rational and analytical about the significance of heritage as a focus of reconstruction. Thus a Lebanese student commented that architects have to take account of heritage issues in planning, not so much for their aesthetic value, but as a symbolic bridge from the past to the present and future: 'Ruins must be preserved because they contain the deep meaning of the tragic past, the frozen moment of pain and torture ... [but] important landmarks and spaces must overlap, linking the past, the present and the future so that we have continuity.'

Most Beiruti students (despite their own comparative wealth as fee-paying students) recognized that social and economic issues are closely related and believed that architects have to speak out and design for all citizens, not just the wealthy. They were critical of the lack of public sector and civil society involvement in many of the case studies they examined, and of the tendency of the architectural profession to pay more attention to the needs of private-sector clients than to broad public interests. Thus, their divided-city manifestos urged increased collaboration between architects and specialists from other disciplines and widespread public consultation as important aspects of recon-struction that should be emphasized by architects when working on post-conflict reconstruction projects. Salient comments from the manifestos follow:

- *Architects have a significant and a moral duty role in re-establishing connection in frac-tured urban environments.* 'It is never too late, it is time to act, to raise our voice and say: save the CBD, save our history and our future' (American University of Beirut student Ali, 2000).

- *Division can be manifested in many ways across cities.* 'The fractures are not always horizontal or vertical' (American University of Beirut student Student, Rami, 2000).

- *The big master plan solution may not always be appropriate.* 'A communal initiative rather than a governmental master plan seems to be the RIGHT WAY where the fruitfulness of major projects is still questioned. Berlin is broke, but the psycholog-ical wall persists'. (American University of Beirut student Fadi, 2000).

A key focus of the design studio process was the use of the Green Line, Beirut's forgotten spine, as a metaphor for planning, in contrast to the 'heart' metaphor used by Solidere. The Damascus Road spine that formed the Green Line is of great histor-ical, geographic and symbolic importance to all Beirut citizens. Focusing the design studio on this area addressed its neglect in public discussion of post-war reconstruction in Lebanon and the subsequent concentration of policy, resources and implementation tools in the much smaller urban area favoured by Solidere. The studio began with an analysis of the 1993 l'AURIF study of alternative plans for the Green Line precinct. This enabled students to identify the opportunities and constraints that the former demar-cation line of Beirut represented. Following the principles identified in their divided-city manifestos, the students worked first in groups and then individually to prepare five design proposals that represented their visions of how architects might contribute to healing the physical and social scars of the Green Line. Projects included:

- *Positive edge.* This project proposed building a 'wall of connection' in which public exhibits and artistic workshops could be displayed, aimed at reviving a multi-level awareness of and in the Green Line, and rendering it as a positive edge: 'Imagine a wall of action: an imaginary wall that takes form through an action verb that best describes it' (Dina and Zeina) (Figure 8.5).

- *The 'E-souk' project* explored connecting the Green Line through information tech-nology programmes across the site, linking the idea of private-sector commerce and commerce with the physical rejuvenation of the area (Bassam).

- *The new Green Line.* This project used landscape as a healing metaphor and proposed 'stitching back the torn fabric' through a sequence of landscape architecture

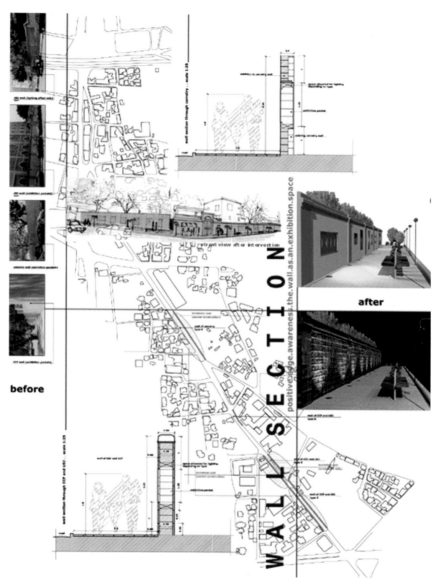

Figure 8.5
THE 'POSITIVE EDGE' PROJECT

proposals: 'Imagine an open space for every citizen, the communication between different communities fostered through open spaces that give the opportunities from people to share rather than to close up their individual, closed, private space' (Julianna and Mark).

- *Linelessness.* This project proposed small, low-income housing and open space projects in contrast to the high-income residential quarters of the adjacent *Centre Ville* precinct. It also investigated low-income residential areas such as Basta, proposing a sequence of smaller incremental interventions. The students' stated aim was 'to solve the problem of the refugees and their illegal occupation of buildings through the creation of housing units dispersed according to the different neighbourhoods' (Nada and Joelle).

- *Mediatheque and media park.* This project proposed a public–private sector initiative combining an electronic showroom of new media innovations with a high tech and industrial 'media park': 'Imagine a joint venture between the Ministry of Culture, the French cultural institutions and the municipality of Beirut' (Fadi) (see Figure 8.6).

On reflection, the Demarcating Lines studio in Beirut encouraged schemes that attempted an innovative rethinking of the former war scar (the Green Line still largely dominating the east–west, Christian–Muslim divisions in the city). The studio's success was, first, in provoking the students (most of whom were too young to have experienced the devastation wrought by the sixteen-year civil war) to think about an urban

Figure 8.6
THE 'MEDIATHEQUE' PROJECT

area in their city that had been largely abandoned, rather than the overused studio site of *Centre Ville*. The second positive outcome was encouraging young Lebanese designers to conceptualize architectural and urban structures to promote coexistence in their own city of Beirut, which is still extensively polarized by ethnic and social division. One of the students from this group actually extended his project into a 'real' project by building a children's playground in the nearby Palestinian Chatilla camp (Figure 8.7). The playground became an oasis of light and hope in an extremely dense residential area close to the central business district, which had been totally left out of Solidere's prosperous vision.

Testing alternative design processes through design, brainstorming and public workshops with young Lebanese architects thus revealed potentially democratic and open methods of using the design process in the reconciliation and mediation processes. This suggests that architects can be trained to rethink their future careers in terms of using their profession as urban mediators and political negotiators, that they can actually effect social change. The teaching process in Beirut also helped me to understand the local critique of the Solidere project. For example, Tracy,[3] a third-year architecture student, wrote:

> Today the government has grandiose plans for a new futuristic city. Mr Miracle is working on rebuilding an entire country for self-advertisement. What Mr Miracle wants to do is remake an entire country. History shouldn't be repeated for Beirut, or any corner of this country that should become like the BCD. Simply, Lebanon is not for sale![3]

Figure 8.7
CHATILLA PLAYGROUND PROJECT

In summary, workshops undertaken with the American University of Beirut students between 2000 and 2002 tested a multidisciplinary approach to the reconstruction planning process. This involved working through design proposals with invited sociologists, historians, lawyers and urban activists. Typical analysis phases were supplemented with more traditional qualitative research methods, such as conducting interviews and public workshops in the still largely destroyed towns outside Beirut, such as Bhamdoun. Choosing as a studio site a largely forgotten zone in Beirut outside the central business district was also a challenging task for students who were familiar with the Green Line but unfamiliar with those living and working on either side of it. This zone was chosen in contrast to many architecture design studios that typically dealt with 'trophy' sites in the central business district, especially the Solidere 'Island'.

The role of architects in the studios was therefore seen more as that of the 'mediator' and 'facilitator' than design 'hero'. The studio process was organized along the following six tasks:

1   *Manifesto and position papers.* The question, 'What is the role of architecture in conflict?' was intended to prompt students to explore the following: what should be architect's role in conflict situations? Do architects have a role to play in 'peace-building' and negotiation between opposing ethnic and social groups? How can we begin to think about stitching back together a divided city?

2   *Undertaking questionnaires.* Part of the studio methodology was asking students to undertake questionnaires on either side of the Green Line to ground their perceptions of the reconstructed Beirut. The students were unused to speaking to such a broad economic and ethnic range of interview participants, and were generally amazed at what they had found out about their city.

3   *Macro and micro.* Looking at Beirut's Green Line as an urban design problem rather than a purely architectural one engaged students in thinking beyond just placing objects in space on a site, to propose long-term cultural and employment programmes across the precinct.

4   *City debates.* Setting up three architectural debates at the university during the semester with invited architects, activists and planners, and providing critiques of the students' work, was successful in opening up debate about the role of architects in fractured zones generally. As invited critic and noted human rights lawyer Ghassan Moukheibir remarked in the final presentation, architects have a moral obligation to act.

5   *Groupwork.* Students were asked to imagine that the United Nations had commissioned them as architects to prepare a master plan for reconnecting Beirut. Working in groups of four, they debated and designed a re-stitching strategy for the city. The group strategy enabled interaction between conflicting views, a clearly

necessary experience for young designers wishing to work in the field of post-disaster reconstruction

6 *Press kit.* The press kit (individual submissions) concentrated the thinking process that emerged from the initial workshop session and exposed positions in a tabloid format vis-à-vis the urban problematic formulated in the position paper and the documentation of the individual's design experimentation. This also had the effect of focusing the designers' thinking on how to present ideas to audiences other than architecturally literate ones.

Finally, the design studio and seminar process also helped me to clarify my own perceptions of the future role of architects in Beirut, as viewed by the important generation of design students soon to enter the profession. Their highly imaginative and often provocative projects enriched my own very limited experience of the city under investigation.

Dividing Line studio III: It is about time? Nicosia, 2002

As a member of the jury I found the whole experience highly educational, not only because I was encouraged to focus on Nicosia as a divided city, but also because it was easier for me to see why some things I would also have probably attempted, are not as sound as they seem when one is immersed in the act of design.[4]

The Nicosia design studio was developed as the third and final fieldwork component in the Dividing Line studio sequence. The student group developed proposals for Nicosia's Buffer Zone (Figure 8.8). The studio was run with urban design professor, Michael Sorkin who involved his Master's of Urban Design students from the City College of New York in the same project. After conducting design studios across Mostar and Beirut between 1999 and 2001, I refined the Nicosia studio brief and method in light of the successes and shortcomings of the previous workshops. For example, much more interaction occurred in our Nicosia studio with local municipality planners and architects than had happened in Beirut and Mostar.

The title of the Nicosia studio, 'It is about time?' referred to issues of space, time and politics. These three components were seen as integral to an understanding of the post-war city and its social practices, especially when the city is subject to urban change or other forms of transition. This situation is well illustrated in the spatial condition of the Green Line in Nicosia, as it was in the example of the two other cases studies of the *ligne de demarcation* (Green Line in Beirut) and Boulevard in Mostar. The political climate, in which both Greek and Turkish Cyprus were applying for admission to the

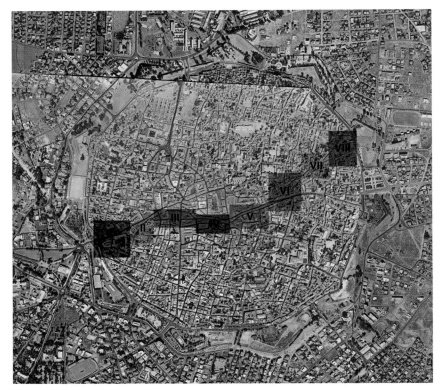

Figure 8.8
THE NICOSIA BUFFER ZONE: STUDIO SITE, 2000

EU, as well as the ageing of the two political leaders of the divide, have spurred a fervent search for settlement to end the 'world's last divided capital'. Using Nicosia as our template, the central aim of the 'It is about time?' studio was to open a discursive platform and design workshop for enlarging the role of architects beyond that of producers of *objets d'art*. The studio instead looked at the design process as provoking architects to adopt into the roles of urban mediators and speculators about how architecture can effect social change in socially contested urban centres.

After reviewing existing design concepts for the Buffer Zone or Green Line through the Nicosia master plan, students investigated design and planning alternatives that could contribute to resolving the physical stalemate of the UN-patrolled 'dead zone'. The challenge, through an architectural dissection of the Buffer Zone, was to then reveal a series of pilot projects for actual consideration by authorities administering Nicosia. This design exercise was particularly timely because, at the time of the studio (April–August 2002), peace talks were being held in Cyprus where the critical issues for establishing a genuine peace solution were reuniting cultural and political territory and removing partition barriers.

Thus, the studio attempted to understand the Nicosia border and its (un)making by using different concepts of time as a form of knowledge. The studio also forged an understanding of the (trans)formation of the border zone and beyond that was not based on the construction of a series of successive and disconnected instants, but on the notion of time as an expanded present. The investigations of the Nicosia studio were also based on two important positions. The first was to abandon the notion that analysis is a separate phase that precedes design and to adopt the idea that there is a continuous process between reading (excavation) and writing (speculation). The second was to take a critical view of the proliferation of abstract drawings and maps that urban design studios often generate and that are influenced by the spaces of representation produced by public authorities.

In summary, the objectives of the Nicosia studio were to:

- understand and respond to the challenge of an undivided Nicosia through a cycle of design 'excavations' and 'speculations' developed across the Spring Semester

- compare and assess a strategy of a transitory and incremental design framework and major interventions demanded by future peace talks across the island

- synthesize relevant experiences acquired from other war-divided cities

- interpret, adapt and re-evaluate relevant architectural and urban theoretical position(s) introduced in the studio programme

- work with local Cypriot architects, planners, residents and politicians in our formulations of design projects.

Having slowly digested some of the complex issues involved in designing for Nicosia, the first design exercise was aimed at a design 'excavation' and producing a 'structure of coexistence'. That is, what was required was an initial intuitive response to the problems and territory at hand via speculation about what could be a building type for coexistence; for example, a museum, a library, an urban park, a memorial? This exercise was intended to promote imaginary and fluid design responses, which could then be further developed as the workshop progressed.

The final outcomes of the studio projects raised many theoretical and practical issues concerning the possibilities of using design as a viable tool for resolution in the divided city context of Nicosia. The studio also helped clarify technical and legal issues surrounding the partition trajectory and the need to remain non-biased when preparing design alternatives for the Buffer Zone. For example, when preparing our brief for the studio, in an interview with the author Madeleine Garlick (2002), an officer with the UN in Nicosia, remarked:

> Whether one agrees with one side or the other is academic. At the UN we advocate use of neutral terms, and this will help you too (and I think will give the students a more balanced view). The better term would simply be bisecting the north (Turkish Cypriot) and south (Greek Cypriot) divided capital city… Note: when we say 'north' and 'south', we use lower case, because it is intended to make clear that no recognition is implied of the division.

The following summary of projects indicates the range of 'reconciliatory' concepts addressed in the 'It is about time?' studio.

The 'Nicosia Development Company'

Student Mustafa based his work upon the Solidere model of a privatized company for the reconstruction and development of central Nicosia (Mustafa, then coincidentally, worked for Solidere). After formation of his suggested development company, the land ownership of the Buffer Zone would be transferred to the company (as in Beirut's

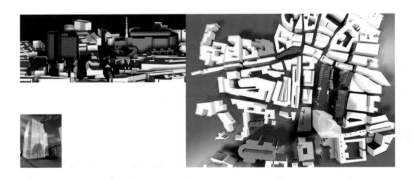

Figure 8.9
REVITALISING THE CENTRE OF NICOSIA: 'THE KHAN' PROJECT

Centre Ville project). Linked to this project was the concept of the 'tourism of devastation', that is, attracting tourism to make Nicosia more economically sustainable. Mustafa's project concentrated his proposed public–private partnership through a 'Khan' project (see Figure 8.9), the Khan being a complex of shared (Greek and Turkish Cypriot) buildings that contain a hotel for transitory visitors, including a commercial zone and offices. The Khan project strategically bridges the Buffer Zone. In this sense Mustafa's project intended to use the building programme of tourism as a mechanism for reconciliation in Nicosia. The proposal was structured along a flexible ten-year timeline, assuming that future changes in land ownership would be substantially eased by the promise of peace on the island of Cyprus.

'Reconstructing the Heart of Nicosia'

Nasri Qumri's project explored the spatial concept of 'delusion'. Delusion was defined by Qumri as an 'erroneous belief that defies rational argument and despite all evidence to the contrary it can also take the form of a psychiatric disorder manifested in conditions such as schizophrenia and paranoia'. The project sought to construct a new 'cultural axis of unity' parallel to the exiting main passage of Ledra Street. The proposed intervention searched for a new way to represent the city, 'a new time with a new spatial experience' in addressing the existing landmarks, religious spots and axes, and how these layers could be used and processed again. Qumri's specific design proposals included:

- a new 'gateway' to the old city of Nicosia

- a European Union head office in Cyprus improving the surroundings of the existing Omeriah Mosque

- new educational cores for tourists 'and all Nicosians'.

Healing Nicosia

One of the students, Imad, developed the idea that healing a divided city can occur by establishing a series of temporary projects or 'points of light'. He suggests that the reconciliation process starts through a 'de-brainwashing phase', in order for the city to evolve as a complete unit. Imad's project is revealed through structures that he sees will enable all Nicosians 'to catch a glimpse of each other's lives without having to deal with established biases and misconceptions'. The architectural manifestation of the project is elaborated through water and reflective panels. The first installation is a reminder of the no man's land of the past; the morphological trace of the Pedios River, which the Green Line actually traces. The reflective panels:

remind us of the mirror that the Turks placed on their land vis-à-vis the Greek bunker on the intersection between the buffer zone and Ledra Street. Maybe after all by exposing and confronting the problem, we could finally get to overcome it and try to learn from the past in order to clear the ground for a better life in the future. Interview with Imad, a student, in 2002.

Discovery Plaza

Student Joseph explored the idea of knowledge transfer in this project. A strategic part of it was the Learning Plaza, a space where all Nicosians could gain access to the public radio, together with a library, museum and auditorium and 'get a reading of the others' way of life and language'. The project was intended to function after the start of the unification process. Joseph commented on his project:

In the end, I do not expect this project to solve the problem, since the problem needs the help of people and not buildings and structures… but the plaza with its buildings is a setting, which could hold the people working at eliminating the problem. In addition, you cannot [predict] how people would use such a space.

The Discovery Plaza project proposed to refurbish an existing government building and adjoining urban spaces in the Buffer Zone, so that it could be used by a bi-communal, local government authority.

Studio outcomes

In summary, the 'It is about time?' studio was a valuable research tool for my investigation of Nicosia. It tested the capacity of young architecture and urban design students to deal with scenarios of political and ethnic instability. Design responses from the students raised during the investigation of Nicosia included:

- How and by whom is an architectural project extracted from the totality of a post-war city situation in order to come up with the programme or brief for a project?

- Is the architectural project to take a specific form in order to facilitate or contain a desired social or political result? Is there thus some kind of prioritization regarding the various domains met in dealing with a complex organism such as the city?

Having reflected upon the design studio in Beirut, I omitted from the Nicosia study a brief dictating what would be finally produced. Consequently, the Nicosia studio created a 'brainstorming' experience for participants, students and jurors alike. The students were expected to assess the specific situation of Nicosia, decide what the goal of their own design should be and come up with a proposal. Each student conse-quently chose a different part of the city to work with. Thus the resulting proposals vary from what could be described as small-scale architecture to grand urban designs, and from quite progressive to rather conservative schemes.

A number of approaches were also adopted in dealing with the peculiar status of Nicosia as a divided city. Many of the proposals that emerged suggested temporary or evolving interventions, acknowledging the need for a transition period between the present and the desired future state of the city. And whereas some students were will-ing to eventually erase whichever physical entity divided the two communities, others felt that history should leave some kind of trace behind. As already mentioned, most proposals contained a strong and inventive concept but not all were necessarily archi-tectural or urban in essence. Apart from mentioning the steep decline in property values from the south to the north of the city, no participant undertook an in-depth study of the possible differences between the two sides and consequently no discus-sion took place on how to deal with such differences.

There also seemed to be a difference or gap in the strength of the concepts and their eventual physical manifestation. This was a common problem in all the Dividing Line studios. The clarity of the central idea was lost on the way many times, perhaps reflecting the difficulty in translating something non-architectural into something that belongs to this domain. This kind of discrepancy was spotted in all stages of the studio process, namely, the initial analysis, the concept and the actual design proposal. In other words, the initial analysis may have, at least partially, been based on non-architectural parameters and the suggested interventions may have had a pseudo-architectural character, with the subsequent effect being of an equally hybrid nature.

Design investigations revealed, therefore, that if the overall goal was to bring the two communities closer together as Cypriots, then the island needs to function as a whole, rather than as two arbitrarily divided halves. Cyprus cannot but be the coun-try of both communities. The island, the city of Nicosia, the neighbourhoods, the squares and the streets are the ground which both communities need to perceive as common. Coming up with a design proposal that will facilitate the proper use of the urban fabric thus seems a valid target for an architectural or urban design proposal. So, while dissolving the effects of the accumulation of ideological differences is of utmost importance and urgency, what will also serve as catalyst for reconciliation is co-presence and co-awareness. This can take place on the level of the street, the square and the city. Hadji Christos (2002) comments in this regard: 'Acknowledging the common ground under their feet cannot but help them see their common humanity, a realization that might put any differences in religious dogmas and ethnic ideologies into a more realistic perspective.'[5]

On reflection, involving Beiruti students in a city officially more divided than their own created a dynamic pedagogical experience and potential for future cultural exchanges. Student proposals which manipulated architectural parameters to bring the two communities together physically, were in the end more realistic propositions rather than those designs which arbitrarily assigned symbolic uses to buildings which were supposed to promote reunification mainly through cultural events To go to a cultural centre, one needs first to be convinced by other equally ideological means that this is the right thing to do – a task that involves non-architectural parameters. A city with spatially dysfunctional pedestrian and vehicular movements cannot adequately serve its inhabitants, however many beautiful, symbolic, social and cultural centres it may have.

Guiding principles

A framework or set of guiding principles to use in future academic investigations of cities split by social, economic and ethnic conflict emerged from the three Dividing Line studios. This framework is intended for adaptation by both educators and professionals working in the field of post-disaster reconstruction, who cannot afford the time and experience of actually living in their particular city under scrutiny. It involves (but is not limited to) nine steps (see Figure 8.10) that are not always sequential, but may provide a foothold to enable architects to operating more effectively in this complicated field.

1   *An analysis of the site* through an urban design survey of opportunities and constraints, context survey (that is, identification of important landmarks, neighbourhood reference points, landscape features and traffic patterns). Brief surveys of existing demographic and ethnic profiles of subject site and locale may also be important at this stage. Archival research of photographs and newspaper clippings may also prove informative. The process of diagramming and collating complex economic and demographic data into usable information is the next critical stage.

2   *Determine functional brief,* that is, what is actually needed – public space improvements, housing rehabilitation, infrastructural upgrade or other – through identifying key stakeholder groups, both local and international, with whom the students and architects will work. Semi-structured questionnaires may be useful in this process to draw out specific questions relevant to the site under investigation. Such a process (as related to post-war cities) can be used to uncover a range of experiences and opinions about the existing situation. The involvement of local sociologists, economists, anthropologists, developers and civic activists may also be useful at this stage.

3   *Proceeding with initial design speculations,* together with onsite analysis and arriving with visions and hypotheses, which the studio or architect may then test with representative political and local community actors.

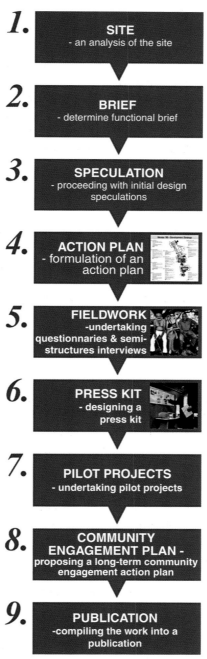

Figure 8.10
DESIGN STUDIO GUIDING PRINCIPLES

4 *Formulation of an action plan* by determining the brief, process, methodology and scope of intervention, based on the findings listed above. Brainstorming, using maps and models to create options.

5 *Undertaking further questionnaires and semi-structured interviews* with residents in the sites under investigation, with more specific questions related to design proposals. Undertaking on-site design workshops to test the initial design propositions.

6 *Designing a press kit* to summarize and promote design proposals in tabloid format intended to be read by the general public.

7 *Undertaking pilot projects* (after consultation) to test the design concepts and philosophies through concrete projects. These projects could include modest conservation or infrastructural, architectural and environmental projects.

8 *Proposing a long-term action plan* by identifying who will develop, maintain and administer the pilot project under consideration over a long-term time frame, for example, for the next five years.

9 *Compiling the work into a publication* for distribution to local and international planning agencies as well as to community agencies, so as to devise a strategy for pursuing the goal.

Targeting young architects through design workshops thus offered a platform for re-engaging in a provocative reconstruction debate. Such research projects could be undertaken in design schools to investigate the social and physical fault lines of all urban centres, from Melbourne to the Bronx. Testing small components of any design strategy through modest pilot projects can also be an empowering exercise for young architects whose prolific butter-paper design sketches are normally disposed of after each new studio project.

The Dividing Line design studios also tested the use of interdisciplinary processes in the design conceptualization stage. It showed that sociologists, economists, lawyers and even doctors could be included in formulating project briefs for future student projects. Their contribution can be amalgamated with local politicians and members of the public in community forums where students discuss their proposals. Two main questions emerge here. First, how can architectural education be oriented more towards the process of building and its impact on society, than towards object-oriented heroic architecture? Secondly, how can architectural education become more consultative? How can we develop the capacity to reach out to other relevant disciplines and target the community groups who will have to bear the positive and negative impacts of the proposed architecture?

In search of socially engaged architects

My investigation of three post-war cities has concentrated upon reconstruction strate-gies in three cities partitioned by war. The demarcating lines imposed by violent conflict became at some point, a 'no man's land', a contested zone where the Green Line divid-ing one ethnic or religious community from another constituted not just a battle line and post-war border, but also a mental partition that kept former neighbours apart physically, socially, economically and, most importantly, psychologically. While the polit-ical backgrounds were briefly outlined, it was not the purpose of my investigation to concentrate in detail on the histories of conflict and division in each city, which are well documented by others referenced in the case study chapters. The long and important relationship between violence, space and cities is already well documented, and as Calame (2002: 45) notes 'speaks to the fact that the city has always been, and continues to be, the manifestation of a social contract between its citizens and its patrons, or state, in which individual liberties are traded against passive, collective security'.

Despite some valiant post-war reconstruction attempts, particularly the bi-communal and interdisciplinary approach used in Nicosia, it is obvious that while lawyers, doctors, engineers and many other professional and non-professional groups have all played significant roles in alleviating the chronic human and physical suffering wreaked by the alarming acceleration of urban conflict, we may still well ask: where are the architects?

It is thus only by looking over the self-defined walls of the architectural profession and out towards the more pressing issues that affect the social and physical health of cities that the practice of architecture can be reinvigorated. Focusing exclusively on aesthetics rather than ethics, on understanding architectural form and its manifestations, rather than on its social implications, has confined architectural discourse within the extremely narrow community of its own professional elite. As Ghandour (2002: 68) remarks, 'By reducing the understanding of society to that of built form, the discipline of architecture has thus dissociated itself from social practice'.

Refocusing the design profession on social and ethical concerns may provide an effective platform for an architectural contribution to reconstructing cities polarized by ethnic and economic conflict. As discussed earlier, the failure of many modernist architects to provide effective reconstruction strategies after the Second World War indicates that aesthetics and architectural heroism alone cannot solve the scars of sustained urban violence. But within a different paradigm it can play a significant role in social reconcil-iation. One way of doing so is by using the design process to encourage opposing ethnic groups to meet, to talk and to reassess their needs, despite the paralysis of a 'peace-making' process. However, finding ways in which architects can actually make a difference in post-war situations has been a critical challenge in my fieldwork. The political issue of trying to get different sides to talk and to agree on a way forward was an immense but rewarding challenge in the design studio context.

I propose that architects can have a significant role in the design and re-assemblage of urban environments partitioned by war and social conflict. This involves a multifaceted process. Architectural education and practice needs to be radically revised so that, first, design professionals adopt interdisciplinary approaches (for example, by collaborating with economists, lawyers and sociologists). Secondly, they operate as mediators by integrating public consultation in their reconstruction planning so that the process of community rebuilding becomes as important as its product. Thirdly, they move away from orthodox methods such as master planning towards the implementation of pilot projects. This accords with Kumar's (1997: 168) argument that 'Shattered communities can only be rebuilt over a slow period of time at a high cost', as this provides time for social as well as physical reconstruction. This incrementalist approach to reconstruction can provide opportunities for architects themselves to rethink their roles amid the imminent increase of global and social catastrophes.

As a result of my post-war investigations, I define architecture and its associated fields as a system of spatial thinking that can be linked both to site-specific design problems and to understanding the city and the region in their specific social contexts and the ways is which these features impact on architecture. This broader definition of architecture extends the role of the profession beyond being the conceivers and executors of blueprint plans to that of potential negotiators and mediators of urban politics and planning.

The concept of architects without frontiers then offers a liberating future to design professionals as mobile, collaborative agents able to work outside traditional sites and constructed environments. Our mission could be to use both the aesthetic and socially transformative capacity of the architectural discipline towards a goal of equitable and sustainable design outcomes. This can be achieved through listening, observing and speculating about modest spatial solutions and working with other professions in the slow healing of communities and cities destroyed by civil conflict.

Notes

1   This studio was co-ordinated with Darko Radovic, Associate Professor at Melbourne University. Many of the Australian students involved in the project were experienced architects and planners, and were studying a Master's course in urban design.

2   Interview with Zijad, August 2000, Mostar.

3   Student, Tracy, Divided-city manifests, American University of Beirut, May 2000.

4   Student, Rita, Divided-city manifesto, American University of Beirut, May 2000.

5   Interview, Christos, architect, Nicosia, May 2002.

Bibliography

Adwan, Charles (2002) Beirut's rebuilding woes. Unpublished paper delivered to City Debates Conference Series, American University of Beirut, 5 June.

Anderson, Mary (1998) *Rising from the Ashes: Development Strategies in Times of Disaster,* Boulder, CO: Westview Press.

Association of Sarajevo Architects. (1989) War architecture, *Magazine for Architecture, Town Planning and Design,* Sarajevo.

Barakat, Sultan (1998) City war zones, *Urban Age,* Spring, 11–15.

Barakat, Sultan (ed.) (2005) *After the Conflict, Reconstruction and Development in the Aftermath of War,* London: I.B. Tauris Press.

Baudoui, Remi (1990) Between regionalism and functionalism: French reconstruction from 1940 to 1945. In: *Rebuilding Europe's Bombed Cities,* J. Diefendorf (ed.) pp. 31–47, London: Macmillan.

Bell, Bryan, (ed.) (2004) *Good Deeds, Good Design: Community Service Through Architecture,* Princeton Architectural Press: New York.

Benvenisti, Meron (1982) Administering conflicts: local government in Jerusalem and Belfast. Unpublished doctoral dissertation, John F. Kennedy School of Government, Cambridge, MA: Harvard University.

Bevan, Robert (2006) *The Destruction of Memory. Architecture at War.* London: Reaktion.

Beyhum, Nabil (1992a) *Rebuilding Beirut and Lost Opportunity,* Beirut: Rami al Khal.

Beyhum, Nabil (1992b) The crisis of urban culture: the three reconstruction plans for Beirut, *Beirut Review* (4):112–114.

Bing, Judith (2002) Ideas and realities: rebuilding in post-war Mostar, *Journal of Architectural Education,* 54(4):3–10.

Bohigas, Oriel (1999) Ten points for an urban methodology, *Architecture Review,* 206(1231): 32–33.

Bollens, Scott (1999) *Urban Peace-Building in Divided Societies: Belfast and Johannesburg,* Boulder, CO: Westview Press.

Bressi, Todd (1993) *Planning and Zoning New York City: Yesterday, Today, and Tomorrow,* New Brunswick, NJ: Center for Urban Policy Research.

Calame, Jon and Charlesworth, Esther (2006) *Divided Cities,* Charlottesville: University of Virginia Press (forthcoming).

Calame, Jon (2002) Commentary on cities on the edge conference, *Architecture Review,* Summer Issue.

Castells, Manuel (1992) The world has changed: can planning change? *Landscape and Urban Planning,* 22: 73–78.

Charlesworth, E. (2004) Beirut: the metaphor of the body. In: *War and Cities,* P. Somma (ed.), Chapter 5. Urban International Press, Newcastle-upon-Tyne.

Cherrey, G. (1990) Reconstruction: its place in planning history. In: *Rebuilding Europe's Bombed Cities*, J. Diefendorf (ed.), pp. 209–228, London: Macmillan.

Cibarowski, Adolf (1956) *Town Planning in Poland, 1945–1950*, Warsaw, Polonia Publishing House.

Cranshaw, N. (1978) *The Cyprus Revolt*, London: George Allen and Unwin.

Crawford, Margaret (1991) Can architects be socially responsible? In Diane Ghirardo (ed.) *Out of Site: A Social Criticism of Architecture*, Seattle, WA: Bay Press, pp. 27–45.

Crisp, J., Talbot, C. and Cipollone, D. (2002) *Learning for a Future: Refugee Education in Developing Countries*, Geneva: UNHCR.

Danner, Mark (1998) Bosnia: the great betrayal, *New York Times Review*, Volume 45, No. 5, March 26.

Davie, Michael (1987) Maps and the historical topography of Beirut, *Berytus*, 35: 141–164.

Davie, Michael (2002) City as excavation? Notes for the excavation of Beirut: a quest for national identity? Unpublished paper delivered to City Debates Seminar, American University of Beirut, 3 June.

Davis, Mike (1993) *City of Quartz: Excavating the Future in Los Angeles*, New York: Vintage Books.

Diefendorf, Jeffrey M. (1990) *Rebuilding Europe's Bombed Cities*, London: Macmillan.

Diefendorf, Jeffrey M. (1993) *In the Wake of War: The Reconstruction of German Cities after World War II*, New York: Oxford University Press.

Dorell, Edward (2003) Closed doors, *Guardian Education*, 29 July: p. 29.

Dyckhoff, Tom (2003) Bob's still the builder, *The Times*, pp. 22–24, 22 July.

Fawaz, Eila (1983) *Merchants and Migrants in Nineteenth Century Beirut*, Cambridge, MA: Harvard University Press.

Fischer, F. (1990) German Reconstruction as an international activity. In: *Rebuilding Europe's Bombed Cities*, J. Diefendorf (ed.), pp. 133–144, London: Macmillan.

Fisk, Robert (1990) *Pity the Nation: Lebanon at War*, London: A. Deutsch.

Foucault, Michel (1986) Of other spaces, *Diacritics*, 12: 22–27.

Friedmann, John (1987) *Planning in the Public Domain: From Knowledge to Action*, Princeton, NJ: Princeton University Press.

Gavin, Angus (1996) *Beirut Reborn: The Restoration and Development of the Central District*, London: Academy Editions.

Ghandour, Marwan (2002) Building as social practice. In: *Architectural Education Today – Cross Cultural Perspectives*, William O'Reilly (ed.), pp. 63–69. Lausanne: Compartements.

Glenny, Misha (1992) *The Fall of Yugoslavia*, London: Penguin.

Goldman, J. (2005) Warsaw: Reconstruction as Propoganda. In: *Resilient City*, L. Vale and T. Campanella (eds), pp. 135–158. New York, Oxford University Press.

Hamdi, Nabeel (1996) *Educating for Real: The Training of Professionals for Development Practice*, London: Intermediate Technology Press.

Hamdi, Nabeel and Goethert Reinhard (1997) *Action Planning for Cities: A Guide to Community Practice*, London: John Wiley Press.

Hasic, Tigran (2002a) Rebuilding regional structures: visions of sustainable urban communities in post-conflict zones. In: *Reshaping Regional Structures: A Northern Perspective*, B. Olerup, L.O. Persson and F. Snickars (eds), Aldershot: Ashgate.

Hasic, Tigran (2002b) Sustainable reconstruction in post-war city zones, *Open House International*, 27(4): 71–82.

Hasic, Tigran and Bhandari, S. (2001) New outlooks on reshaping and revitalizing post-conflict regions: strategies, principles and models for reconstruction, unpublished paper presented at the 41st Congress of the European Regional Science Association (ERSA) Zagreb, 21 August.

Healey, Patsy. (1995) *Managing Cities: The New Urban Context*, Chichester, J. Wiley.

Hewitt, Kenneth (1997) *Regions of Risk: A Geographical Introduction to Disasters*, Harlow: Longman.

Hocknell, Peter (2001) *Boundaries of Cooperation*, London: Kluwer Law International.

Holden, C.H and Holford, W.G. (1951) *The City of London: A Record of Destruction and Survival and the Proposals for Reconstruction as incorporated in the final report of the planning consultants, presented in 1947 to the Court of Common Council*, London, Architectural Press.

Hughes, Robert (1980) *Shock of the New*, London: BBC Press.

Ignatieff, Michael (2003) A bridge too hard, *Weekend Australian Magazine* 19 January: 16–19.

International Crisis Group (1999) *Is Dayton Failing?* ICG Reports, No. 80, Brussels, International Crisis Group.

Kabbani, Oussama (1992) *The Reconstruction of Beirut*, Prospects for Lebanon 6, Oxford, Centre for Lebanese Studies.

Kabbani, Oussama (1998) Public space as infrastructure. In: *Projecting Beirut: Episodes in the Construction and Reconstruction of a Modern City*, H. Sarkis, and P. Rowe, pp. 240–259. New York, Prestel.

Khalaf, Samir (1993) *Beirut Reclaimed: Reflections on Urban Design and the Restoration of Civility*, Beirut: Dar an-Nahar.

Khalaf, Samir and Khoury, Philip S. (1993) *Recovering Beirut: Urban Design and Post-War Reconstruction*, New York: Brill.

King, Anthony (1990) *Urbanism, Colonialism and the World Economy: Cultural and Spatial Foundations of the World Urban System*, London: Routledge and Kegan Paul.

Kumar, R. (1997) *Divide and Fall, Bosnia in the Annals of Partition*, London: Verso.

Ladd. B. (1997) *The Ghost of Berlin*, Chicago, IL: University of Chicago Press.

Lang, Peter (1997) *Mortal Cities*, New York, Princeton Architectural Press.

Lefebvre, Henri (1996) *Writings on Cities*, Oxford: Blackwell.

Lewis, James (1998) Survival, reconstruction and vulnerability, *Settlement and Reconstruction of Post-War Settlements*, Workshop report, York: Institute of Advanced Architectural Studies, University of York, 16–18 May.

Logan, Bill (1996) Hanoi after the bombs. In: *Urban Triumph or Urban Disaster – Dilemmas of Contemporary Post- War Reconstruction*, S. Barakat, J. Calame, J. and E. Charlesworth (eds), York: Institute of Advanced Architectural Studies, University of York, pp. 35–50.

MacGinty, Roger (2001) Ethno-national conflict and hate crime, *American Behavioural Scientist*, 45(4): 639–653.

Maiwandi, Ajmal, and Fontenot, Anthony (2002) Re-doing Kabul, *Open House International*, 27(4): 41–49.

Makdisi, Jean Said (1990) *Beirut Fragments: A War Memoir*, New York: Persea Books.

Marcuse, Peter (1999) 'Dual city': a muddy metaphor for a quartered city, *International Journal of Urban and Regional Research*, 13(4): 697–708.

Marshall, M. and Gurr, T. (2003) *Peace and Conflict 2003: A Global Survey of Armed Conflicts, Self-Determination Movements, and Democracy*, College Park, MD: Center for International Development and Conflict Management.

Merrifield, Andy (1997) *The Urbanization of Injustice*, New York: New York University Press.

Müller-Hegemann, D. (1993) Die Berliner Mauer-Krankheit. Zur Soziogenese psychischer Störungen, Herford (in German).

Nasr, Joe (1996) Beirut–Berlin: choices in planning for the suture of two divided cities, *Journal of Planning Education and Research*, 16: 27–40.

Ockman, J. (ed.) (2002) *Out of Ground Zero*. New York: Prestel Publishing.

Papadakis, Yiannis (2001) Nicosia After 1960: a river, a bridge and a dead zone. In: *Zypern. Gesellschaftliche Fffnung, Europdische Integration, Globalisierung*, Gisela Welz and Petra Ilyes (eds), Notizen, Frankfurt: Kulturanthropologie.

Perez-Gomez, Alberto (1983) *Architecture and the Crisis of Modern Science*, Cambridge, Mass., MIT Press.

Plunz, Richard (1998) *New Urbanisms: Mostar*, New York: Columbia University Press.

Purcell, H.D. (1969) Republic of Cyprus, *Cyprus: The Problem of Perspective* (Nicosia: Public Information Office).

Putnam, R.D. (1991) The prosperous community: social capital and public life, *The American Prospect*, 13.

Putnam, R.D. (1995) Bowling alone: America's declining social capital, *Journal of Democracy*, 6(1): 65–78.

Rowe, P. (2002) Professional design education and practice. In: *Architectural Education Today – Cross Cultural Perspectives*, William O'Reilly (ed.), pp. 25–41. Lausanne: Compartements.

Rowley, Alan (1994) Definitions of urban design: the nature and concerns of urban design, *Planning Practice and Research*, 9(3): 10–18.

Said, Edward (1994) *Representations of the Intellectual*, New York: Vintage Books.

Salaam, A. (1994) The reconstruction of Beirut: a lost opportunity, *AA Files*, 27, Summer: 11–13.

Salaam, A. (1998) *Reconstruction of War Torn Cities*, Beirut: Order of Engineers and Architects Publications.

Sarkis, H (2005) A vital void: reconstructions of downtown Beirut. In: *Resilient City*, L. Vale and T. Campanella, pp. 281–298. New York, Oxford University Press.

Sarkis, Hashim and Rowe, Peter (1998) *Projecting Beirut: Episodes in the Construction and Reconstruction of a Modern City*, New York, Prestel.

Sarkis, Hashim (1993) Reconstruction reconsidered. In: *Recovering Beirut: Urban Design and Post-War Reconstruction*, Samir Khalaf and Philip S. Khoury (eds), New York: Brill, pp. 101–126.

Sassen, Saskia. (1999) Whose City is it Anyway? Lecture at the American University of Beirut, March 19.

Scott Brown, Denise (1990) Urban Concepts, London: *Architectural Design*, 60(1/2):18–20.

Scott-Ball, M. (2004) Expanding the role of the architect. In: *Good Deeds, Good Design: Community Service through Architecture*, Bryan Bell (ed.), pp. 132–140. New York: Princeton Architectural Press.

Smith, Adam (1998) *The Wealth of Nation,* Oxford Paperbacks.

Smith, Helena and MacAskill, Ewan (2002) Cyprus again, *The Guardian*, 16 January, pp. 5–6.

Somma, Paola (2002) War and Cities, *Open House House International*, 27(4): 3–10.

Sorkin, M. (2003) *Starting from Zero*, New York: Routledge.

Sorkin, M. and Zukin, S. (eds) (2002) *After the World Trade Center*, New York: Routledge.

Stewart, A. (1991) Healing the Wounds, *Building*, 256(51): 34–38.

Strand, H., Wilhelmsen, L. and Gleditsch, N.P. (2003) Armed Conflict Dataset, International Peace Research Institute, Version 1.2a.

Tabet, Jad (1998) From colonial style to regional revivaism. In: *Projecting Beirut: Episodes in the Construction and Reconstruction of a Modern City*, H. Sarkis, and P. Rowe (eds), New York, Prestel. 83–106.

Tanaskovic, Darko (2000) unpublished paper delivered to War and Cultural Heritage Conference, University of Venice, April, 2000.

Till, Jeremy (1997) The knowledge of architecture. In: *European Architectural Education: Managing and Measuring Diversity*, John Worthington and George Cairns (eds), York: Institute of Advance Architectural Studies, University of York, pp. 107–112.

Trawi, Arman (2003) *Beirut's Memory,* Beirut, Banque de la Medeterrance.

Tueni, Ghassan (1998) From the geography of fear to a geography of hope. In: *Projecting Beirut: Episodes in the Construction and Reconstruction of a Modern City*, H. Sarkis and P. Rowe (eds), pp. 285–295. New York, Prestel.

Tueni, Ghassan (1992) Beirut our city, *An Nahar*, 2 February, pp. 8–9.

UNDP (1984) United Nations Development Programme, *Nicosia Master Plan – Final Report*, Nicosia.

Ungers, O.M. (1997) *The Dialectic City*, Milan: Skira Press.

UNHCR (2005) United Nations High Commissioner for Refugees, UNHCR News, 3 January. Available on-line at http: //www.unhcr.ch/cgibin/texis/vtx/tsunami?page=news&id=41d9772e4 [accessed 21 January 05].

UNOPS (1995) United Nations Office of Project Services, *The Nicosia Sewerage Project: A Plan for Nicosia, a Strategy for the World*, Nicosia.

Vale, L. Campanella, T. (2005) *Resilient City*, Oxford University Press: New York.

Voldman, Daniele (1990) Reconstructor's tales: an example of the use of oral sources in the history of reconstruction after the Second World War. In: *Rebuilding Europe's Bombed Cities*, J. Diefendorf (ed.), pp. 16–30. Macmillan, London.

Watson, Sophie and Bridge, Garry (2000) *A Companion to the City*, Oxford: Blackwell.

Watson, Sophie and Gibson, Katharine (1995) *Postmodernism and Spaces*, pp. 254–264, Oxford: Blackwell.

Wigley, Michael (2002) Insecurity by Design. In: *After the World Trade Center*, M. Sorkin and S. Zukin (eds), pp. 69–86. New York: Routledge.

Wise, Michael (1998) *Capital Dilemma: Germany's Search for a New Architecture of Democracy*, Princeton, NJ: Princeton Architectural Press.

Woods, Lebbeus (1998). *Radical reconstruction*, New York: Princeton Architectural
    Press.
Worthington, John (2000) The changing context of architectural practice. In: *Changing
    Architectural Education*, David Nicol and Simon Pilling (eds), London: Spoon Press,
    pp. 27–40.
Wright, Gwendolyn (1991) *The Politics of Design in French Colonial Urbanism*, Chicago, IL:
    University of Chicago Press.
Yarwood, John (1998) Rebuilding Mostar, *Town Planning Review*, Special Studies, Vol 3.
Yayha, Maha (2000) Comments (unpublished) to Cermoac Conference, Beirut, March 11.
Yiftachel, Oren (1995) The dark side of modernism: planning as a control of an ethnic
    minority. In: *Postmodernism and Spaces*, Sophie Watson and Katharine Gibson (eds),
    Oxford: Blackwell, pp. 216–242.
Zimonijic, V. and Tanner, M. (2003) Available online at http:
    //news.independent.co.uk/europe/story.jsp?story=431924 *The Independent* (London)
    9 August 2003.

Further Reading

AJ (1940) Total war and the next years, *Architects Journal*, 23 May: 519.

AJ (1941) Thoughts inspired by the first meeting of the RIBA Reconstruction Committee, *Architects Journal*, 26 June: 413.

Akar, Celina and Mansour, Joelle (2000) What if? Unpublished paper delivered to Divided City Seminar, Beirut: American University of Beirut, 30 March.

Akhal, Fakhry (2000) Divided-city manifesto, Term paper, Beirut: American University of Beirut.

Akinci, M. (1989) *Cyprus Weekly Magazine*, no. 1, November: 13.

Barakat, Sultan, Charlesworth, Esther and Calame, Jon (1997) *Urban Triumph or Urban Disaster-Dilemmas of Contemporary Post-War Reconstruction*, Institute of Advanced Architectural Studies, University of York.

Benvenisti, Meron (1986) *Conflicts and Contradictions*, New York: Billard Books.

Bollens, Scott (2000) *On Narrow Ground: Urban Policy and Ethnic Conflict in Jerusalem and Belfast*, New York: State University of New York Press.

Castells, Manuel and Hall, Peter (1994) *Technopoles of the World: The Waking of 21st Century Industrial Complexes*, London: Routledge.

Corporation of Coventry (1945) *The Future Coventry: Some Proposals and Suggestions for the Physical Reconstruction and Planning of the City of Coventry*, Coventry: Coventry Corporation.

Corporation of Coventry (1966) *The Traditions of Change and Continuity*, Coventry: Coventry Corporation.

Corporation of London (1944) *Reconstruction in the City of London*, London: Guildhall.

Demetriades, Lellos (1998) The Nicosia master plan, *Journal of Mediterranean Studies*, 8(2): 169–172.

Harbom, Lotta and Wallenstein, Peter (2005), Armed conflict and its international dimensions, *Journal of Peace Research*, 42(5) 623–635.

Hourani, Albert (1995) *The Emergence of the Middle East*, Berkeley, CA: University of Califironia Press.

International Crisis Group (1999) *Is Dayton Failing?* ICG Reports, No. 80, Brussels, International Crisis Group.

Khalaf, Samir (2002) Culture and resistance, unpublished paper delivered to City Debates Seminar, American University of Beirut, June.

Le Corbusier, E. (1965) The city of tomorrow and its planning. In: *The City Reader*, Richard Legates and Frederic Stout (eds), London: Routledge.

Lefebvre, Henri (1985) *The Production of Space*, translated by Donald Nicholson-Smith, Oxford: Blackwell.

O'Reilly, William (2002) *Architectural Education Today – Cross Cultural Perspectives*, Lausanne: Compartements.

Papadakis, Yiannis (1993) The politics of memory and forgetting, *Journal of Mediterranean Studies*, 3(1): 139–154.

Republic of Cyprus (1967) *The Second Five-Year Plan (1967–1971)*, Nicosia: Planning Bureau.

Republic of Cyprus (1994) *Report on the Demographic Structure of the Cypriot Communities*, Nicosia: Press and Information Office.

Sarkis, Hashim and Rowe, Peter (1996) *Open City: Rebuilding Downtown Beirut's Waterfront*, Cambridge, Mass., Harvard University Press.

Vestbro, D. (2002) Global housing problems and the role of professionals, available online at URL: www.inesglobal.com/publication/ines_proceedings/WORKSHOP_1HTM/VESTBRO.HTM, [accessed 12 October 2005].

Wigley, Michael (1995) *The Architecture of Deconstruction: Derrida's Haunt*, Cambridge, MA: MIT Press.

Zeino, Bassam (2001) Reconsidering reconstruction, unpublished paper, Divided Cities seminar paper, American University of Beirut, March.

Index

(*Italic* page numbers refer to illustrations)